THE LOST COLONIAL BOY

A journey through a life of drama
and adventure in England and Malaya

ALAN GILL

Mereo Books

2nd Floor, 6-8 Dyer Street, Cirencester, Gloucestershire, GL7 2PF
An imprint of Memoirs Books. www.mereobooks.com
and www.memoirsbooks.co.uk

THE LOST COLONIAL BOY

978-1-86151-983-2

First published in Great Britain in 2021
by Mereo Books, an imprint of Memoirs Books.

The address for Memoirs Books can be
found at www.mereobooks.com

Mereo Books Ltd. Reg. No. 12157152

Typeset in 11/15pt Century Schoolbook
by Wiltshire Associates.
Printed and bound in Great Britain

Contents

∼

Acknowledgments

Chris Newton

Editor in Chief, Mereo Books. A huge thank you for his guidance, encouragement, patience and kindness. At the time of publishing we had never met. I was in Canada/USA and Chris in Gloucestershire, UK. The Covid Pandemic had created a new world but Chris surmounted the roadblocks. *www.mereobooks.com   www.chrisnewton.co.uk*

Jenn Best

Artist, Life Coach, Friend. Technical/Computers skills, organization and artistic talent were key elements in navigating the mine fields of communication during the Pandemic and liaising with the Editor and Publishers across the Atlantic. Thank you, Jenn. *bestjenn01@gmail.com*

Ivy Pan

Illustrator. With thanks for creating the Maps and assisting on the cover. *ivypandesign@gmail.com*

Peter Chester

Old Coathamian. Author "New Lamps for Old" for his permission to use images from his book regarding the old School. Books available on Amazon and Goodreads.

King's Own Royal Regiment Museum, Lancaster.
Image of HMT Empire Windrush 1947

Writers' Group, St. Petersburg, Florida

An eclectic coalescence of wonderful people, who encourage and support each other and share their stories. Thank you for tour support and encouragement over the years.

Introduction

Christopher Ondaatje's book *The Last Colonial* is riveting not only for its title, which spells finality, but with its very personal memories and vivid descriptions of a world that was inhabited by many of us, a world that nurtured us and is now past, as are the lives of many it emboldened. His stories of youth and life in Ceylon (Sri Lanka) struck close to home for me, evoking clear thoughts of my own youth and childhood growing up in Malaya (what is now Peninsular Malaysia) before its independence from Empire. Ondaatje's stories have driven my own search for the world absorbed and lived in by my father in the 1940s and 50s, in Africa, India, Burma and Malaya, the latter being the place where we shared life together. It is in part a story of another age; an age forgotten, or perhaps not, as it shaped the lives of many of us and created experiences and memories that drive us still. There is a siren call to that world.

Into the second decade of the twenty-first century there is a mantra that tells us "sixty is the new forty". Better health, better options in life, better travel, easier living conditions, improved fitness, instant communication and connection are all ours for the asking. But in paying lip service to these offerings from the table of plenty, I have a different view. In my generation many of us have not lived that safe "cradle to the grave" life offered up among the victory spoils of the Second World War and other wars; spoils provided from the banquet of death and destruction. Some have taken a different path, perhaps dominated by the wanderlust instilled from the lost days.

It is only as I grow older still, with more years behind me than ahead, that I search for the things that shaped me; but it is more than that. It is also the search for the experiences and knowledge and humanity of the personal lives of those closest to me. What is genetic and what is experience driven? What of my parents and grandparents, their early lives, world wars and other battles; the fight to survive through rationing of food and fuel and the loss of life itself on the home front, sicknesses, poverty and the ultimate success in rising from the ashes; a world reshaped and the old order lost and yet they had lives lived with dignity and passion?

Memories are beginning to create a perspective. So I go down memory lane not out of trepidation but with the joy of discovering anew the world I inhabited a lifetime ago.

My inner self has always been haunted, a strong voice always calling, by the Malaya of the 1940s and 1950s. That lush tropical country, its rains, and the seemingly endless canopies of trees and grasses of every shape, size, twists and turns, occupied by and protecting loud colourful birds, the home of flying lemurs, gibbons, tigers, snakes and lizards, all of which are more present in my appreciation now, rather than as a young boy when one was so fearless and part of that nature. The peoples of that Eden were part of the mystique; Malays, Chinese, Tamil, East Indian, European, Eurasian and other mixes; Muslim, Buddhist, Hindu, Christian. Did we see any of those demarcations? Not at all, and I am fortunate that gift of ethos has been with me all my life.

Our youthful bravado never considered that in Malaya there was a military and police operation against the Malay communists and bandits, with deadly skirmishes won and lost. Friends came and went, some suddenly as they had lost their fathers in that small war that surrounded us, but that too became an experience of life and really did not deter the call of our paradise

I seek my answers in the shape of vignettes which will bring those years back to life; those seeds that were planted and defined my life. Within my soul, I know I will always be that lost colonial boy. That I treasure and pay homage to those that allowed me entry into that world.

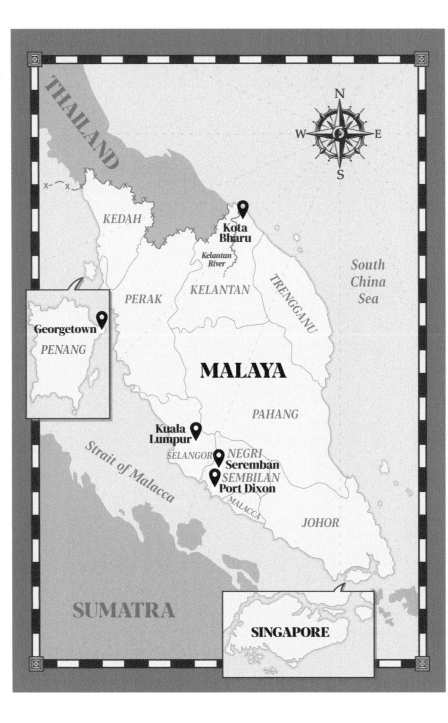

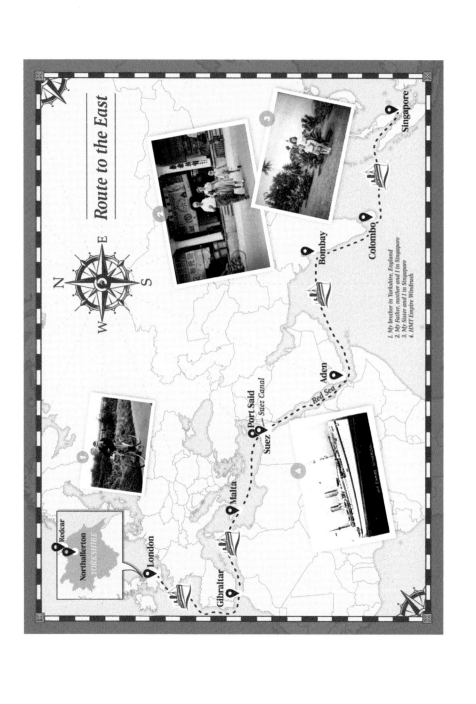

Route to the East

1. My brother in Yorkshire, England
2. My Father, mother and I in Singapore
3. My Sister and I in Singapore
4. HMT Empire Windrush

CHAPTER 1

THE EARLY DAYS

My mother, Maud May Gill, born in 1909, was five feet and half an inch according to her passport, and in reality not even that, but she was a giant of a woman. She was the eldest child of seven born into a family of good British coalmining stock from a small village in County Durham in north-east England. My grandmother, Ellen Gittins, was also the daughter of a coal mining family; Grandfather George had made the journey from the coal mining mountains and valleys of Wales.

Grandma Gittins, striking and very tall at five foot nine plus, was a strong, imperious but compassionate woman of great fashion. She ruled any room she entered; she was the centre of attention and energy. It was not only her impressive height and well-poised figure that drew attention; her clothes and panache completed the picture. The darkness of Queen Victoria was gone; there was an enlightened Edwardian world shining brightly, and fashion was in play with the working class. Grandma Ellen would noticeably have a silk brocade or satin blouse and short ruff at her neck and a short-waisted coat, colourful, with coated buttons on the sleeves and on the front. Her jacket would be left open, the days of constraint being over. Tall as she was, Grandma Ellen's skirt was long, yet not too long to show her shining heeled leather boots, which were tied with perfectly-spaced leather laces. She was a striking figure indeed as she walked between her friends and admirers to take her hallowed seat at the corner of the bar. Her four young daughters always had a hand, willingly or not, in pressing her clothes, helping her dress and polishing her shoes.

Grandad George, a stern taskmaster at work, was not of the hierarchy but one of those who made things happen, a leader in a dangerous industry. Yet he was a gentle man and of much smaller stature than his wife; he was content in her admired shadow. They were a caring and formidable team. He would join her on these evenings, attentive to her as she perched erectly on her corner stool, reserved by right, and then he would move away to spend an easy evening with his fellow miners, sharing tales of life gilded with good strong northern ale and the clink of glasses. These evenings, mainly Friday and Saturday, were a joyous time in these small, bonded communities in low-ceilinged rooms filled with laughter, conversations of new life and sports. For a moment the dark and dangerous coalface and sudden injury or death were locked away, hidden behind the cloud and soothing haze of cigar, pipe and cigarette smoke.

It was on these nights that for a few moments time stopped. It was ethereal. Breaths were held, hearts raced for everyone within hearing distance when, without announcement, Grandad George, the diminutive Welshman, in his high-collared starched white shirt, cuffs and cuff links showing, newly-pressed black suit and high waistcoat with requisite silver fob watch and chain, would glance across the room at his wife. They smiled their smiles. He would stand and then unleash the most magnificent, soaring and mesmerising tenor voice that ever came out of the valleys of Wales. Unaccompanied, this celestial voice of such purity, a gift, brought tears to the eyes of the hardened coal mining men as the last note was held and then quietly died and there was silence. Granddad George would turn and meet the eyes of his wife, and smiles were exchanged. Conversations resumed for a while as George Gittins took a small sip of his newly-poured ale, just enough to wet his lips, and then silence fell once again as that first tenor note, soaring upwards, unlocked the doors of heaven and the coal miners' world was filled with song, light and hope. To all who had heard him, that voice was never silenced.

By the time Maud Gill was thirty-eight she found herself in one of the farthest outposts of a crumbling British Empire, my Malaya. It was an experience totally out of context to what she must have expected in life, coming from that small, safe, closely-knit community, but one for which she had been unknowingly prepared. She lived through the First World War, a young pre-teen girl, finished school at 15 and then went on to work in the retail trade and then as a nurse's aid, Higher education was not an option, for many cultural reasons. She met and married my father, Charles, in what today is still a rich market town, Northallerton in North Yorkshire. All was idyllic for the young couple for a number of years.

Charles Gill, born in 1907, was the eldest of five children of John and Agnes Gill. The family lived in one of a simple row of brick cottages, with no indoor plumbing and three small bedrooms. The house, under this powerful paternal grandmother's eye was immaculate but sparse in its available comforts. She was another diminutive but powerful woman who ruled with an iron fist throughout her life. John Gill, the grandfather I never met, served in the First World War with his two brothers and carried on his trade as a builder on his return from the hell they all experienced in France; some were gassed, some wounded.

The five children got the usual basic but good education and were essentially working full time by the time they were fifteen. My father worked in a grocery store that would become a small successful chain in the North East of England, a connection through my grandmother. The control of that connection was cruel enough to provide some assistance, but only sufficient that it did not enable the Gill family to move beyond its presumed station in life. Grandfather John Gill was killed while the family was still young, having fallen and broken his neck whilst on a building site. But the boys kept working, Granny Gill took in laundry (all hand done), and the family made do. My father won an opportunity to go to Britain's Naval Academy but the "Family", owners of a chain of grocery stores and also closely connected to the aristocracy for centuries, the side that could still wield influence from a distance in those days, intervened. They refused to advance money for uniforms etc and decreed that Charles would continue to have a position in their local store.

In short, all the "boys" had interesting lives. Edward became a master tailor and spent his whole life with one company in this craft; Arthur became what we would today call the Chief Operating Officer of a large municipality in Wales; Jack (John) stayed in his home town and was employed by a battery supply company.

Jack had an interesting story. Before the Second World War, he was called upon to repair aircraft engines at various airports in England; he was one of the few who had the skills for this task. A new gentleman showed up one day to work with Jack and he held the lowest rank possible, Aircraftsman. He was a quiet man, a loner, kept to himself and seemed troubled. This man was known as Aircraftsman Shaw, a pseudonym granted so he could escape his broken life and his hells of war and torture. Aircraftsman Shaw is probably better known to the world as Lawrence of Arabia. His request for his insular life was respected by my uncle.

Charles Gill, my father, whose stories are more entwined with the early part of my own life appears later in the various vignettes that form this book.

Granny Gill would continue to wield a lot of power over the boys in her life. It had been a hard life for her, but she had no complaints, and she commanded the respect of all who crossed her path.

CHAPTER 2

CLEANLINESS IS NEXT TO GODLINESS

Granny (Agnes) Gill, the Matriarch – 1878-1962

Cleanliness is next to godliness.' That particular phrase is not specifically written in Holy Scripture, but if it were then surely I have seen, smelled and touched the Promised Land. Cleanliness in all its glory.

My paternal grandmother, Agnes Gill, was born in north-east England in a little coastal town, Tynemouth, in 1878. She was married in the town of Northallerton, North Yorkshire, to John Gill, the grandfather I never knew. They had five children and six grandchildren who also called that idyllic place home. My own father, Charles, the eldest son, was born in 1907. The other three boys also had regal names: Edward, Arthur and John. My aunt inherited her mother's name, Agnes.

The family lived in brick row housing in a sheltered cobblestone walk that connected two streets. Five rooms, three up, two down, one and a half storeys, no basement or back door. Four boys in one room and the daughter with the parents. No running water or toilets. Access to fresh water was across the cobblestones to a communal tap shared by four families. Their toilets were also communal in that they were all together, spaced over a running stream that connected them to a sewer; however each family had its own space, with each door being locked on the outside by large padlocks. No need to flush. That communal space was immaculate with each family scrubbing and cleaning to keep the scenery fresh, new and healthy. The entrance steps were polished and honed with yellow stone. Cleanliness!

Grandfather John had done many labouring jobs and had also worked in horse stables, but was at his best as a master bricklayer. Granny Gill, as she eventually became known to her children as well as grandchildren, had been a house companion, maid and nurse's aide. The children were well looked after and respected in town, and by their early teens were essentially in full-time employment in the usual infrastructure of a small market town. The brothers and sister had a great loyalty to each other from their earliest days.

The small home was kept pristine and functional, everything in its place, cleaned, washed and ironed. Carpets were taken out and beaten every week. Granny Gill may not have had much, but she had pride, and her children were firmly brought up; they would not disappoint her.

The First World War came and went and touched this small family with its throttling fingers. Grandad John Gill survived the hells of France, as did his brother Ernest. As they were brothers they did not serve in the same regiments, the military playing the odds that separation may alleviate losses to a family. Both survived, although Uncle Ernie, as he was known to all generations, was one of the many gassed in trench battles and suffered all his life. The greatest loss for the family came in 1927 when my grandfather fell off a ladder while laying bricks, broke his neck and died a few days later.

What to do? This was not the time of social services safety nets. The boys had all been working in part-time jobs and with school finished by the ages of fifteen or sixteen they were starting to apprentice in a number of trades: grocery stores, hardware stores, tailoring. Granny Gill had contacts and decided to take in laundry from the upper classes, limiting her services to just a few clients. The small kitchen, the smallest of the four rooms in the row house (real address Number 4 New Row) became the laundry room. There was an additional stove to boil water, carried from across The Row, and the main fireplace in the living room was put to use on laundry day.

Water was poured from the one common tap into shining metal buckets (perhaps one was white enamel), by Granny Gill, all four foot six of her, and carried across the cobblestones to her small house. A laundry tub and wringer were put to use. The only mechanical part was the wringing machine where the rollers were turned by hand, mainly by Granny. No dryers! Clothes rinsed in separate tubs were taken out to two clothes lines, previously washed down and not too close in case of entanglement. Lines were fixed from the high brick wall across to the hooks on to her own part of the family row house. Wooden props raised the lines and laundry and the breeze was allowed to waft through. People walking through New Row would dodge the obstacle course of lines of laundry.

Drying was watched carefully; too dry can create extra work. Clothes were taken in, slightly damp, neatly folded or hung for more selective drying in front of a coal fire. The whole house took on a fresh scent of pure air wafted down from the North York Moors or from the eastern side, carrying the saltiness of the North Sea. All mixed in a special elixir, still treasured to this day by those of us who have been privileged to live in that part of heaven on earth. There were two irons on the go, heated by the fire, and the ironing began in the evening; lighting was by gas lamp.

The boys laboured for their mother and passed all their earnings on to her, and the family succeeded. The 'boys', as they were always known, still helped her as they moved on to different parts of the country. She was the lynchpin; they were always in touch by letter and came home twice a year. They could not and would not miss; the Matriarch called. Her pride in presenting herself well was instilled in them all, and they did not let her down.

I can remember as a child and then a young boy walking to Granny Gill's on a laundry day. Her heavy days of taking in laundry had long gone, but there were still sheets and towels and so on, even when she lived alone on her later years. I can still see the cottons and linens, propped on their lines, really a singular line and only half filled, shimmering in the breeze. Cleanliness was still alive. On entering her home there was that whole new level of freshness, pure oxygen. My senses can be stimulated to this day just by the thoughts of walking to see my diminutive grandmother; truly a giant.

Granny Gill's next-door neighbour of almost sixty years was Mrs Martin, a widow from the First World War and a lady who had no children. Their friendship was quiet, private and respectful; there was no intrusion. The odd errand would be run if someone was sick; perhaps if one was passing by the butcher's shop they would enquire if there was something for their neighbour and so on. Mutual, quiet respect and unheralded caring were always in play. They had one other thing in common, and that was their mutual pride in the presentation of their homes. Weekly the thresholds of their front door steps were scrubbed and honed. The rounded edges would be reddened, or sometimes they would be yellow or white; not a speck of dust in sight, even though exposed to the elements. It was a time-consuming job but both ladies would be down on hands and knees scrubbing away. Cleanliness meant respectability.

Even after decades of seeing each other virtually every day, the two widows would share their daily greeting, in their local dialect, which would go something like this:

"Gran' mornin, Missus Martin."

"Aye, it looks grand. Are thee well then, Missus Gill?"

"Can't complain, Missus Martin, can't complain."

"That's grand then."

All was well in their world. Simple needs were met. To these ladies cleanliness meant respectability. If these jewels of the north did not have much in the way of "brass" (in the Yorkshire dialect, brass means money or wealth), they made up for it with their respectability. Cleanliness!

The lower windows of their homes, one in the kitchen, the other in the living area, were small-paned and of the thicker glass typical of those built in the late 1800s. Light came in through the swirled glass and in part some privacy could be maintained through its thickness. The window panes and white frames sparkled, up and down. No smears or marks left for criticism, no grandchildren's fingermarks; we knew our place.

For each of the chores there was a prescribed day. The weather had to be fought in the winter for the right to wash and dry, but if ever there was a wind it was always a good drying day; God's breath. We always knew where Granny Gill would be on a specific day; laundry Monday, steps and windows Tuesday. Bustling market days in the town, enshrined by centuries of tradition, were Wednesdays and Saturdays, and shopping was also done on these days at the traditional bakers and butchers. Tuesdays and Thursdays could also be days for visiting grandchildren in town.

A lady of vigour, determination, autocracy and a caring strength, Granny Gill was known to all the established storekeepers and owners. She was greeted courteously by name even if just passing by. She always wore a coat and I never saw her with it unbuttoned, except for the hottest days; a hat or freshly-pressed headscarf finished off her wardrobe. Her small heeled shoes probably pushed her to the magnificent height of four feet seven inches. She may not have had much, but she was always well presented.

On the few times I accompanied her as a young boy or teenager, I treasured the greetings she would receive as she walked along the High Street. Men on the pavements or standing in their storefronts would raise a hand to their foreheads as they nodded their respect and say something like this, in their quiet, dour, yet sincere ways:

" Grand mornin' Mrs Gill. Well, are we?"

"Well enough, Mr Thomson. Well enough. Nowt to complain about." (Nowt meaning "nothing", in the Yorkshire dialect).

"This young lad must be your Charlie's son? Spittin' image he is, nay doubt abaht it."

"Aye, he's a gran' lad alreet".

My shoes were clean, socks straight, sweater and pants matched, hands and face were clean. I am sure I made her proud.

Cleanliness was certainly next to godliness for this woman we all revered and whom the small market town respected. These are memories firmly etched in my mind. I can still see the row house, the cobble stones; I can smell the breeze and the market odours, the clean and busy streets and the smiles of respect from the shopkeepers.

When I revisited this birthplace of mine in September 2017, the High Street and the Wednesday market were replaying the symphony of old. Thomson the Butchers (close to New Row) was still in business, into its fourth generation, but had just sold out to a private company. It was late in the day, and the store was not busy but it was being scrubbed down by diligent staff, all in their blue striped butcher-aprons. As I entered I received friendly greetings, shared that I was just passing and recalled Butcher Thomson's. Some still remembered the old Butcher Thomson, the kindly man who doffed his cap to my grandmother. They were sad to see the last of the family selling up after so many years. Good Yorkshire folk!

Buttressed close by is the All Saints Anglican Church, a magnificent sight with its bell tower. Foundations from the 7th century still exist in parts of the church, as do major stone walls constructed in the 9th and 13th centuries. It was our family church, where baptisms, weddings and funerals took place. My father and mother were married there, my sister, brother and I were baptised there and Granny Gill and Grandfather John are close by in the Cemetery. To this day the church grounds and adjoining cemetery have immaculate grounds. Granny Gill is surely at rest there.

Across the street is the Porch House, an old historic house and inn that was built in 1584, some parts of it even earlier. King Charles I was a guest there in 1640 and made a return visit in 1647 as a prisoner. My wife Carolyn and I stayed there in 2012 and 2017 as guests, not prisoners. Our room was that originally used by the King.

The small homes on New Row are gone, but the row is still an active passage and walking route between major streets. My parents' old house, some ten minutes walking distance away and over a hundred years old ,is still in existence and well kept.

My 2017 visit allowed me to breathe in the pure and nostalgic air that provides the scent of memories and lets us know we are home once again in God's Own County. Cleanliness and godliness in one.

CHAPTER 3

JOURNEYS TO THE EAST

Close to the mid-point of the twentieth century, I would make what I called my oriental journeys, like some defiant great explorer of old. The journeys were book-ended by England and Singapore. It is not lost on me that the symbol of England is the noble lion and the meaning of Singapore, in Sanskrit, is Lion City.

In the late 1940s my mother took my older sister Jean and me out of the embracing, safe cocoon and beauty of North Yorkshire to start out on a journey to an unknown land some eight thousand miles away. There I would rekindle my love for my father, the man of whom I had no memory. He had continued his military duties of World War 2 in Africa, India and Burma in another arena, Malaya, fighting in a communist insurgency. The Malay Emergency, as it was known, was a bloody war that lasted twelve years. It was far, far away and just a few years after I was born. We were to leave by ship, the *Empire Windrush*, destination Malaya, landing in Singapore.

Gerald, my older brother by eleven years, was to stay behind in England to continue his education. Still impressed on my memory, etched in black and white, is the view of him standing in the dim grey light on a cold January morning on the long, desolate platform at the train station in London, waving goodbye until he was lost in the steam and shadows. Some three years later we repeated the separation dance when he again waved farewell to us after we had been on leave in the UK for a few months. Then, twenty years later, another indelible but darker picture manifested when he waved me the final goodbye on the day I emigrated to Canada. That last picture, scored, or scarred, into my very being in the gallery of my mind, was the last time I saw him alive. He was killed three months later by a car. That is another story.

Over the next eight years I would take this Oriental journey to and fro four times. My first treasured atlas with shadings, contours, graphs, symbols, numbers, lines thick and thin, had a lot of pink countries, the latter signifying the British Empire that was and is no more. It became well-worn as I traced the lines of my journey. To see these dots, our ports of call, on a map was mesmerising. The dots grew with greater meaning and interpretation on each voyage. They would lie still, folded in sleep, until poked awake by a small finger, and were magical in conjuring up expectations from earlier visits. On later journeys my father, pipe in hand, would gently point to a place on the map and say "that is where we are." There would be another dot, the next point of call, and the quiet phrasing explained: "That's where we are going to be in a few days." Calm expectations were created of what I might see, but not too much was given away as my father believed that the experience itself would paint the true picture. His incredible knowledge and story-telling would complete the canvas. These masterpieces are still engraved in memory.

It was hard to immediately conjure in my mind how I

could be on a ship and that ship was taking me to a dot. But as the journeys progressed, and with my father's guidance, my experiences became memories and then points of reference which allowed me to create life around the dots. They were living things like small buds waiting to burst open with their treasures. What people would I see at the next dot? What clothes would they be wearing? What sorts of boats would be in the harbour? What smells would come from the cargo being loaded? Would there be children? What would we see when we went ashore? What different aromas would greet us, and would we be able to speak the same as these new people? And so the questions went on. Incredible visions and mysteries had been opened up to me, all under a gentle guiding hand. Today I pursue my travels with the same excitement and innocence as that young boy. I may have figured the dots out, but I still relish and savour the innocence and surprise of the search and give thanks for the shared opportunities of the past. I was safe then and feel safe now.

Those early journeys we made are really bundled into one whole adventure that lasted close to a decade, a period that etched itself into the very fabric of my being. The voyages, some coming, some going, three with my father accompanying us, and of course the growth of participation, learning and understanding, created an appreciation of all things new and different. Experiences create our future.

The First Journey

From the 1940s onward the most common route to Asia was through the Suez Canal. We left England, sailing through the ever roiling, troubling Bay of Biscay and stopping off in Gibraltar as we entered the Mediterranean; I remember the vast Rock, but of course Gibraltar's famous monkeys were my highlight. From there the *Empire Windrush* made its way through the Mediterranean, passing Malta and onto my first new continent, Africa.

Our first port of call as we sailed between Africa and Europe was Port Said in Egypt. Here the ship would refuel, take on and unload cargo and restock certain provisions, especially water. It was also an opportunity to leave the ship and explore another culture. For us, this did not happen on the first trip, as my father was not with us. This period in time was the start of skirmishes which many years later would develop into a war over the Suez Canal and borders, led by Colonel Abdul Gamal Nasser, the eventual President of Egypt. It was my first sight of the military flexing muscles. On one side the French had control and on the right bank the British were on show with their armoury and troops. Calls of "Get your knees brown!" greeted us as we waved at the gallant young men as the ship made its way slowly to the great Salt Lakes and out into the Red Sea to the next port of Aden in Yemen. There were sights of the Pyramids, farmers working on the banks desperately trying to create a small oasis of survival and sights of the noble beast so critical to their lifestyles, the camel.

The canal was minute compared with what it is now and our ship was a ridge in a crocodile line composed of a mix of vessels as we snaked down to Aden. The ship occasionally stopped in some smaller lakes while another small convoy would wend its way north. The ships all carried cargo, as trading was still the driving force.

Our next "dots" on the map were in the great sub-continent of India, Bombay (now Mumbai) and Colombo in Ceylon (now Sri Lanka).

At this point, as a young explorer, I had already traversed the English Channel into the Bay of Biscay, one of the fiercest storm regions of the North Atlantic, through to the safety of

Gibraltar, sailed the Mediterranean, reached the Gulf of Aden via one of man's greatest achievements, the Suez Canal, and plied the great trade routes of the Arabian Sea and the Bay of Bengal. Then on towards Asia and down through the Malacca Straits between Sumatra and Malaya to the safe anchorage of Singapore at the southern tip of the Malay Peninsula. I had the advantage of sailing via the Suez Canal, but surely I must have counted myself amongst those intrepid explorers who framed some of my learning: Vasco Da Gama, Columbus, Magellan, Raleigh, Drake and Captain Cook, the latter from my home county of Yorkshire. And now at last Malaya, my home for the next eight years and in truth the country whose spirit and blood still course through my veins. I call her 'Mother Malaya'. And there to greet me was the gentle and guiding warrior, my father.

In all we made that ocean journey four times, twice out and twice back. Some of the little dots gained greater significance in time and the famous pins on the map of the British Empire shrank, as did that dynasty. Young as I was, memories were forged. Understandably I believe I have rolled the shipboard experiences into one, but childhood and youth can be forgiven. I could not say what happened on what particular trip, but I believe memories are better ingrained by the experiences when I was in the company of my father.

Port Said with the ancient, powerful, life-giving River Nile of myth and history, the core of civilization, was a cauldron of activity. In Port Said we left the ship and our family of four wended its way through crowded, noisy streets, the air full of the pungency of spices, oil and tobacco. Even noisy, stinking, drooling camels were led down the streets; quite a sight for me, as I had probably thought of them as just the mythical beasts you see with Jesus on Christmas cards. People brushed together, shouting in loud, passionate languages with beguiling rhythms.

Shopkeepers, jostling in the bazaars, thrust their wares at our small, inquisitive family, each pleading with hand over heart that their goods were better and cheaper than others. When their passionate overtures became too strong, my father quietly stepped forward. He let us learn before intervening. With the more persistent and invasive he simply kept his pipe in his teeth, smiled at the same time, made eye contact and shifted his jacket (he did not wear a uniform) just enough to attract attention and show the handle of his gun. We moved on freely after a friendly "Salaam". I can still see this place and certainly would recognise it today with its boisterous cacophony of bartering, colours and smells.

The greatest joy my sister Jean had was a special treat prepared for her by my father on each occasion the ship went through Port Said and the Suez Canal at night. Always knowing the captain of the ship, he had arranged for two deckchairs to be placed on the ship's bridge late in the evening. This was for their most spectacular private showing of the Pyramids as the ships quietly glided by. Huge, ancient monuments, they were not obscured by the invading lights of the megacity that exists today; they were lit only by the light of the moon and the reflective vastness of the skies.

The ship glided slowly down the narrow canal, sand on either side, in silence; there was just the gentle throb of the engines, which you felt rather than heard. The ethereal scene was printed forever in memory, especially as the moonlight subsided and gave way to the golden orb of the sun at daybreak. Who has seen those pyramids in such glory? My sister reminisced on this in October 2019 and our amazement was renewed as our memories were refreshed.

The ship exited the Great Salt Lakes down through the Red Sea where it empties into the Gulf of Aden. We stopped off briefly in Aden, now Yemen, and all I can recall is a sandy, dusty and dull landscape. I am sure it was more than that, but it was not a place for us to enjoy.

Then it was on to noisy, busy, energetic, pulsating Bombay, across the Arabian Sea. That vast city is now Mumbai; named, some say, as a reversion to the original name after the goddess Mumbadevi. In any event the name change did in part eradicate the connection to the old British Raj. Bombay was a huge port, ships of all types and sizes, with some trading ships still under the power of sail. Tenders worked their way out to the ships in the harbour and replenished them with fuel, water, food and goods for trade; some merchant cargo was also off-loaded onto the tenders. The non-stop movement was seemingly chaotic, but the orchestration succeeded with the cooperation of the pilots, the ship captains and the harbour police. The circus of life was there for all to see.

Leaving Bombay and going south down the western coast of India, the next stop was Colombo in Ceylon, today's Sri Lanka. It was a smaller port which seemed even more cramped than Bombay but with the same accompanying orchestra of sights, sounds and smells. This was the last refuelling before crossing eastward over the Bay of Bengal and Indian Ocean, across the top of the island of Sumatra and then south down the west side of the Malay Peninsula to the island city of Singapore. In those days Singapore was a British Crown Colony. This magnificent city republic is now totally independent, having metamorphosed through those difficult post-world-war years, being part of the new Malaysia and then not, to become a beacon to the world.

I had arrived. Seas, miracle canals and oceans had been conquered. I had crossed from Europe to Africa, the sub-continent of India and now into Asia. Singapore, my stepping stone to Mother Malaya, my new home, welcomed me, and there to greet me with his quiet compassion was my father, the man of whom I had no memory but whose warmth and kindness I immediately absorbed. This was the beginning of a love story that I live every day.

CHAPTER 4

Upriver in Kelantan, Malaya, with Bill Bangs

Viewed from the perspective of my six-year-old eyes, Bill Bangs was a giant of a man. Six feet tall, he was slim but broad shouldered, with skin like bronzed and hardened leather, and had an easy charisma and power, all with a gentle welcoming smile. This was the Bill I first saw on the banks of the Kelantan River in north-east Malaya. He greeted our small boat, somewhat larger than a sampan, after my father had brought my mother, older sister Jean and me, plus the one boatman, on a long day's ride upriver from Kota Bharu, Kelantan. Ostensibly this was a social visit with family and old friends.

My father had known Bill for a number of years. Bill was a source of constant military intelligence for decades in Malaya's wars, covering the devastating and ruthless Japanese invasion of the Second World War and the current bloody communist terrorist assaults on local civilians as well as the military. At the time of our journey there was an unwritten understanding that women and young children were off limits; that was to change within a year or so.

Our landing was near Bill's home on a large rubber plantation. The house was raised in the traditional Malay manner, built of magnificent teak, a mirror of the man, and the many rooms were a testament to Bill's eclectic tastes. There were hunting and tribal collections, wood and ivory carvings, kerises (the indigenous wavy dagger/sword in a wooden sheath), silk paintings, colourful batik screens with coverings interwoven with silver, and on a wall a magnificent Japanese sword collection. In one of the living rooms, placed next to each armchair, were small dark grey tables about two feet high that looked like tree stumps with their tops smooth and off-white. At the base there were small outcrops of what could have been polished wood. As I took that all in, I realised that these were the stumps of elephant legs. They had been collected from elephants the workers had found that had been poached and killed by traders, or else from rogue elephants that had destroyed trees in the plantation and villagers' crops. They were a danger. This collection was part of the cycle of life and not as a result of hunting as a personal pursuit. Bill, who had seen enough death of the most torturous kind inflicted by his fellow man, revered life and protected his workers on the estate.

What small boy wouldn't feel he was in the greatest place in his world; an ever-present sense of adventure, a new world to conquer? Yet this one was safe, as his father was by his side. I was the master of all I surveyed on that long journey up river, sitting in the prow of the boat, the first to get to wherever we were going. There were promises of crocodiles, snakes, jumping fish, water buffalo, sightings of monkeys, elephants and tigers and even of mysterious tribesmen, the Orang Asli, in the shadows, who might stealthily come down to the river. Who was I to know that some of these hopes and images were created for the mystery and adventure of a young boy and some may not have even been relevant to that geographic paradise? There is no doubt it was paradise; to me, it still is.

It was here that I learned to tap for rubber. A walk into the plantation, the workers with us, revealed rows of trees with small tin gathering-cups strapped close to the bottom of each. A narrow continuous crevice had been cut into each tree, gradually spiralling, twisting and turning down its own hill, and dripping out at its end into the tin bucket was a whitish, tacky solution. Latex! Something on which the modern world depended and on which family empires had been based, drip by drip. With help I was allowed to carve my own channel in a tree, one which was probably not even ripe for use and not much taller than me. It didn't matter. I was now a rubber planter and the next Bill Bangs!

Among Bill's collections were long bamboo blowpipes as used by the hunter-gatherers in the jungle. These people were rarely seen and were nomadic, but they had a trust of Bill's people; they were an indigenous Malay tribe. The blowpipes were of all sizes, all taller than me, and the weapon was completed by darts about a foot long and with poison on their tips. The darts were held in thick hollowed-out bamboo tubes, capped off by a woven, patterned top. The tube was carried over the shoulder or belted at the waist. I remember the cotton-like padding at the bottom of the tubes on which the darts rested. Some form of curare poison was on this padding and this immobilised the prey. I ended up with one of these sets and even in my teens and back in England I still couldn't hit a bird or rabbit. I would not have survived by hunting, but as a rubber planter maybe!

Stories of tigers were told and there were some skins around the house with magnificent heads that still seemed alive and fearsome. I was promised a tiger hunt, not knowing that the tigers were not hunted and the only time they were taken was when they had become a menace through stalking and attacking people in the kampongs. Or a tiger might have grown too old to hunt in his natural habitat or been forced out of his territory by a rival, thus making him a threat; such was the order of the world.

We set out on the periphery of the estate, really just a short walk for everyone else, but embellished to create an adventure for me. Joining us were quite a number of Bill's people, some with rifles and others with parangs, a sort of machete. A shout from some of the men took us over to the edge of the jungle grasses and there they were, tiger footprints! Could I have had a greater thrill? The walk continued slowly, with more caution. As we turned there were more prints, larger still and moist. This time there was real concern. We were all herded into a tighter circle with the men forming the outside cordon, eyes and guns ready. There were more tracks as we continued to the house and for the next few days there was a lot more vigilance around the big house. But now I had it all. I was a big-game hunter; what a dream!

Bill Bangs had been in Malaya since the late 1920s working in various parts of the peninsula but finally settling in the Kelantan area in the north. He totally immersed himself in the cultures of Malaya and was fluent in Malay, Tamil and into that mix we could throw Chinese and French, apart from his native English. No wonder he gave such great value to the British with his extended intelligence network. He was trusted and respected by the Malay people, no matter what their ethnic roots. He worked hard to improve their world with better working conditions, hygiene, opportunity and pay; this was not just limited to his own estate. On that estate Bill eventually had only Malay workers; he liked their way of life, their quietness, respect and he certainly related as a fellow Muslim.

When we knew Bill, he had already converted to the Islamic faith and lived by its broader frame. He had, as is required of all devout Muslims, completed his "haj" to Mecca, some time in the early 1950s, and he even took his closest worker with him, a man of loyalty for close to 50 years. While known so well to all as "Bill Bangs", a living legend in his own right, Bill was also known by his Muslim name of Mohamed Yusuf. Terms of respect also added to his allure by gracing his name with the terms "Haj" and "Dato". The first speaks for itself and the second is the respectful title of Elder, most often conferred by the Sultan of the state.

At my first breakfast I overstepped the Muslim etiquette relating to food. We were all seated in the magnificent long dining hall; behind each chair, well turned out in their traditional Malay clothing, were the young men responsible for our individual welfare. Apparently the large choice of fresh local foods and fruits was not exactly to my liking but, ever the gracious host, Bill enquired what they could prepare especially for me. It must have been like the Dickensian Oliver Twist/Fagin moment, "Please sir, I want some more!" My request was for eggs and bacon; the latter of course would never be on the menu in this good Muslim household. I am sure my eggs and toast were perfect, but the bacon was missing! So I learned a little etiquette with generous graciousness from our host and friend Bill Bangs.

As the world lurched into war in the 30s and 40s, while maintaining his main role as a successful rubber planter, Bill took on other tasks. He had connections over the Thailand border, organised Malay volunteer groups to assist in the fight against the encroaching powerful Japanese armies and was the first to let the British know when and where the Japanese were going to land near Kota Bharu, Malaya. Some of that latter advice was ignored, to the detriment of the British. Bill continued to be a thorn to the Japanese until he was finally taken by them and incarcerated in the infamous Changi Jail in Singapore.

Bill Bangs' life in Changi was more difficult than for most, and that was hell enough. He was not a member of the surrendered armies, so he did not get what little protection that warranted; he was a known agitator and worst of all, in the eyes of some of the Japanese, was a magnificent specimen of a man who towered over his captors. This persona went with him as he, like so many, was sent to the Death Railway in Thailand and Myanmar (the old Siam and Burma). One Japanese officer took personal exception to that physical presence which they found hard to break down and exorcised his own shortcomings of stature by beating Bill on an almost daily basis. Any lashing is torturous, especially one with a bamboo cane wielded with personal, bullying hatred. Toward the end of the Occupation and the ultimate surrender of the Japanese, the cane was replaced by a long sword. Bill's scarred back was still a testament to that.

Almost 75 years after those events, we can be sure the lives of all the participants are over. All we have are the oral histories. My father, Bill's confidante, knew the ending of the Changi Jail incarceration and tortured life he endured. The Japanese officer died by his own sword, but not by his own hand in the time-honoured bushido tradition. Bill had exorcised his own demons and that sword, the sword of torture and then of retribution, was among the collection on the wall of the Long Room in Bill Bang's Teak House, by the Kelantan River.

Bill never married; he remained on his rubber estate, a generous and respected man who improved the lives of so many of his fellow Malay people. He was a part of our lives for a number of years. He is still remembered fondly by me and my sister who, as she turned eighty-five, started a conversation with me about Bill Bangs with "Do you remember when...?" Yes, we remember and treasure those memories and friends of another age that are indelibly a part of us.

CHAPTER 5

THE PEARL AND THE EGGCUP

The pearl

Nil nocere": do no harm. A very simple statement, often associated with the Hippocratic Oath, which sweepingly covers ethics, reverence, mythical gods (or are they?), knowledge, care of others, judgements, sacraments, faith and the gift of healing, all with the spirit of Hippocrates hovering above. Is that always foremost in a doctor's mind, a part of who he is?

In the hell that was Burma in World War 2 in the 1940s Charles Gill, my father, was once again serving his country, having been in Africa and India. It was in Burma that he received his Officer's Commission in the field of battle; a rare event. The fighting and the atrocities of that campaign scarred many for the rest of their lives, either long or short; man's inhumanity to man had this as its hell; a hell, which for many, burned within for the rest of their lives.

It was here that my father met a young officer, a doctor. While there was no time to build a friendship between these two officers in the traditional sense, they survived, and had some common ground. Both came from North Yorkshire in England, my father from the market town of Northallerton and the doctor from a family farm close by in the Yorkshire Dales, that part of the northern piece of England fondly called "the big sky country and God's half-acre." The doctor was the son of parents who had farmed there all their lives with the cultivated, traditional hope that the son would take over their farm while they retired and, as was common at that time, continue to live in the same home. There were no siblings. The son returned home, with no physical scars, to the protection and challenge of farming. Is there anything that could be more healing than being at one with nature? My father continued his military career in England and South East Asia.

In searching for the essence of a man, it is often the later years that reveal the truths, the infinite courage and the effects of life's battles won, but in reality lost. News came to my father that the doctor had committed suicide. The parents, bereft, had lost their hopes and dreams of the future, living out their well-earned old age, with a son who had returned from the abyss of war in that arena where death stared you down everyday. Fate damned that well-earned future. My father called on the parents and shared with them the valiant and unselfish work their son had carried out, the immense respect all the force, whole and wounded, had for him and the sorrow that all felt in knowing he could not reap the peace so valiantly earned. There is no doubt in today's parlance that PTSD (post traumatic stress disorder) was the destroyer of this young man.

During the visit, the mother insisted that Charles Gill take a gift, not only as her appreciation for his sharing the goodness of their son's actions but in the comfort she felt in knowing that there had been a friend in Burma. He had not been alone. There was no family to inherit this necklace with three large pearls at its centre. It had been given to her by her son on his return from Burma. The pearls were refused, but in the end the mother prevailed, by accepting the caveat of my father that she would have the pearls and necklace appraised and then he would buy them at that price. He said the family gift would be respected by his own family. That was done, and the grieving parents were happy that the gift from their son had passed on to a family with the same core values as their own.

The necklace, which appreciated significantly in value, took various forms over its lifetime until only one pearl was left. The first two had been sold at different times and had been used to help pay for the university tuition of my older brother, who was at medical school. That is certainly a circle of miracles. My own education in England, in later years attending the same school as my brother, where we were both boarders, was in part funded by the second pearl. As for the third pearl, I have pictures of my mother in Malaya wearing evening gowns at various events, and her jewellery was a simple statement with that one remaining pearl as the centre of a simple pearl necklace.

It is said that the jungle warfare in Burma against the Japanese was amongst the worst endured by the soldiers of all races, in one of the hellish theatres of war. Injuries were horrific, and wounded men could not readily be taken out of combat zones, nor could they always keep up with their own troop movements. There was always fear of capture by an enemy, not known for its compassion with the wounded. There were stragglers and some who could not even be carried, and there were no safe havens; this was Hell. Suffering would be even greater on capture; death would not be easy. Our doctor occasionally slipped back to care for those left behind and where he saw that their existing pain and wounds were impossible to bear, that life was held on a short string, he provided peace and comfort in doing what he could for these men; they died with dignity and freedom from pain, at peace. Who are we to judge? We will never be put in that position, the gods willing. The doctor, when free from war, knew he had done the right thing for these men, and yet within his own psyche he could not cope with those memories of the final acts of grace, so war took another casualty.

His legacy, through his gift of pearls to his mother, was that another doctor could take his place. Gerald Gill, my brother, crippled with polio in his youthful prime at 13, completed his medical degrees at Durham University. He in turn had been driven to the gift of healing, influenced greatly by the care he had been given over the years by amazing medical teams; being crippled by polio was not going to slow down his payback, in his own wonderful yet short life. "Nil nocere."

The eggcup

Fast forward to 1951 and the Gill family (less the eldest son) were living in Port Dickson, Negeri Sembilan, Malaya. We lived in what we called "The Big House", formerly occupied by Senior Officers of the Imperial Japanese Army and before that the rich merchant class.. The house, on the top of a hill, was reached by a curving and circular driveway from the main road. Its gardens were essentially left in their natural state with indigenous flora, cleaned back slightly to create an inviting openness for inquiring minds and cared for by our gardeners. I remember the tamarind trees with their long bean pods, the resting place for the tribes of monkeys that walked with authority across the driveway and then rested or indulged their screaming play among the shaded branches.

A common sight around these homes occupied by the military families was the visit several times a month by a "barang" man plying his trade ("barang" being the Malay word for goods or chattels). The Malayan barang man had his woven baskets slung across his shoulders, causing him to tilt as he carried them. There were pots, pans, trinkets, ivory carvings, jade, pewter, woven fabrics, intricately-carved wooden boxes and even silver chalices and knives. The contents would vary, as would the stories, which were part and parcel of the sales and gave a life to the whole experience.

One particular day, my mother looked down the long, winding driveway and saw the barang man slowly shuffling his way upward, the baskets hanging at each end of the long bamboo poles. all weighing him down. This man was different; his climb up the hill was slower, purposeful and determined, but his angled body slowed him. My mother waited, watching the man and the wares get nearer. Close to five feet tall (she put five feet and half an inch on her passport), she was a feisty woman, protective of her family and home but with great compassion behind her steely will. She waited and waited for the barang man, recognised his determination and also something special in his gait, something very familiar to her; her visitor had polio.

Greetings were exchanged, she guided the man to the shade of the car porch and had him sit down so he could get his strength back to display his wares; fresh iced water and cool fresh coconut milk were served. We learned his name was Aziz. Pride of place in his display were the hand-crafted silver objects, carefully wrapped.

During the conversations, Aziz finally asked my mother if she would hire him and if he could design silver for her. She said she had no need of more silver and trinkets. She in turn asked if he could cook; the answer was no. Given some of his physical limitations, doors probably closed very quickly on Aziz; his lot in life was not easy. But the English Mem surprised him. She said she needed a new cook and if he wanted the job he could have it and she would teach him everything she knew. This from a lady whose meals and baking were legend; I can still taste her baking. And so Aziz joined the Gill household, where the numbers of people we employed and housed were greater than needed, but that was part of the caring shown by my mother and father. In her later life Maud Gill remembered Aziz fondly, with his graceful shuffle, and gave him the accolade that he probably turned out a better cook than she had ever been. Who would have thought that a Malay silversmith could make better Yorkshire pudding than the little English lady chef who taught him?

Eventually, as the communist-terrorist offensive, which we lived through, wore down and independence was on the horizon for Malaya, the British pulled back. Our family were no different and would ultimately move to the island of Penang, that Pearl of the Orient, while my father continued with the intricacies of his work on the mainland. Charles Gill believed we had a strong obligation to the people who, while working for us, had been a part of our experience and part of our family. I had grown up among these Malay, Chinese and Indians and their own extended families. They were generous with us and had shared their country, customs and affection. Their ways of life and the time shared at the Big House are indelibly etched in my soul to this day; for that I am grateful.

My father's care for Aziz is typical of his own quiet kindness and respect for others, and reveals to me why he was so warmly welcomed by people of all cultures. The cook was really a silversmith at heart. In that trade in Malaya, shops were set up where individual silversmiths would work together, purchase a chair for a fee, and then lease that space on an ongoing basis for many years. They were able to deal with custom orders as well as share the small retail space. The town of Malacca, not far from our Port Dickson home, had been a commercial powerhouse for free trade for over 600 years. Its glory days, as a settlement on Malaya's west coast, goes back to the trading empire of the Ming dynasty and it was cultivated by Arabs, Indians, Persians and finally the Portuguese. It was in itself a great civilization, the epicentre of the Malay/Muslim blended cultures of faith and education. That was the place to be.

My father, well connected locally and welcomed, as well as looked up to, by the Malay people, took Aziz to Malacca. He negotiated with a well-known jeweller, "purchased" a chair for Aziz and paid forward his lease for a number of years. Aziz could now pursue his true calling and be secure for the rest of his life.

But the story doesn't end there. Just before we left Port Dickson for Penang, Aziz, now a man with a lighter load, came up the driveway one last time with his own inimitable shuffle to say his goodbyes to his extended family. He had a gift for my parents, who in turn had given him skills of independence as a cook anyone would love to hire; that was capped by his true calling by working his magic with silver. He was very proud of his new creations, crafted, perched on his own stool, in the silversmith's store in Malacca; a place that secured his place in his rapidly changing world. The gifts, two beautiful and intricately-designed silver eggcups, crafted from his imagination and with his hands, were used by my parents in their later years, no doubt kindling fond memories as they sat across from each other. These eggcups still hold pride of place on a mantle in my sister's home 70 years later.

Pearls and silver may be treasured, but it is the good karma that flows from man to man, seen in many a story, that is the true treasure of life. My Malaya certainly gifted her karma to me.

CHAPTER 6

THE HEALER AND THE WHISPERER

The Malay Emergency, a real bloody war, between 1947 and 1960, and the Korean War, 1950 to 1953, were part of the framework that influenced my early upbringing. In truth my eight years in Malaya gave me experiences which I treasure to this day. Growing up in that exotic land I am grateful for having been able to share in the cultures of the Malay, Chinese, East Indian and Indigenous people and a mixture of Europeans and their beliefs, politics, families and history, all at the ground roots level. That life is in me still.

The Korean War most of us know about, but the Malay Emergency is something different - or is it? In fact it was a war. Having been ravaged by the Japanese in World War 2, Malaya found itself in another war, with all that brings: death and destruction. Malaya was rich in natural resources, a world leader in rubber and tin backed up by coal, iron ore, bauxite, manganese and so on. The word "Emergency" was employed strictly for the trading and insurance market. In the great monied insurance market that was London, insurance would cover losses of stock, equipment, buildings if there was a riot or other civil disruptions. But a war negated such claims. Everything was lost. So the powers that be declared that this 13-year-war would be called an "emergency"; it allowed life to go on in towns and villages and business to continue as much as possible.

Unfortunately the change in name did not reduce the massacres, murders and torture. Close to nineteen hundred Malay troops and police and Commonwealth troops were killed in this Emergency. Seven thousand communist guerrillas lost their lives and another four thousand surrendered.

Following his distinguished service in World War 2 in his homeland of England, Africa, India and the living hell that was Burma, my father, Charles Gill, was seconded as part of a special force that was formed to begin the fight against the destructive communist terrorist front that had risen in Malaya. That special force was Force Ferret, a specially-selected unit with some legendary history coming out of success in Burma under the leadership of "the soldiers' soldier", Field Marshall Viscount William Slim, known to all as Bill. My father had resigned his Officers' Commission immediately after the War but was sought out by Bill Slim to be a leader in Malaya, so once again he was in the military serving his country in Asia.

My mother, my older sister Jean and I arrived in Malaya 1n 1947, my brother having been left in England for his education; that was the way it was done. Our accommodation, no matter where we were in those years, was good and surprisingly safe. We were well tended to by those working in our homes, and in a way we became part of their extended family. I was particularly lucky as people from other cultures, Malay, Chinese, East Indian, cared for me, shared their customs and language. What a gift of an education.

There was another side to the coin. The jungle where the war and skirmishes were being fought was a moveable hell. The jungle canopy was dense, and there was no daylight; the war could not be fought from the air. There was nothing in sight except steaming jungle, unforgiving, impenetrable. Malay and Commonwealth forces, the latter staffed in many cases by conscripted young men, 18 to 22, from the United Kingdom underwent their baptism by fire in these conditions. An unseen, experienced local enemy well trained in guerrilla warfare, many having honed their skills against the Japanese, added to the fears. Days and nights were spent thigh deep in swamps, small streams or rivers. Snakes were dangerous and the ever-clinging and sucking leeches covered the body. Accompanying all this was the drone and lightning strikes of mosquitoes, day and night. You were never dry. There were constant threats of an ambush, bamboo spiked traps on the small pathways, an enemy around the next bend, wire strung across trees in the night, or the slowly strangling movement of the hidden ones surrounding you in the darkness of day. No forgiveness.

Further north, in Korea, the blood bath continued clenching its jaws of fear and death, and was fed by the same virgin conscripts as in Malaya. After patrols many of these young men were paralysed with shock and fear. They soldiered on, as there was no choice. They were damaged. Today we would recognise this as PTSD but in those dark mid-century wars we knew nothing. We had not learned from "the war to end all wars".

There were many visitors to the Gill home in Port Dickson, Negeri Sembilan. The Big House, formerly built by a wealthy Chinese businessman pre-World War 2, had also been annexed by senior officers of the Imperial Japanese Army, and was now our home. It seemed there was a constant stream of young men at dinner; civilian clothing in place, no uniforms. The nourishing and soothing meals had been prepared by our cook, Aziz.

The young, quiet men in from the jungle and an occasional one from the death strip from Korea were made to feel comfortable and were able to relax for a few days in these settings. Their world consisted of being pampered with hot baths or showers, nourishing food and rest, clean sheets, a large garden in which to stroll and inhale a kinder nature. They had no duty other than to soak in the care that was being given, and then it was a return to barracks. Another straggling cohort would arrive, drifting in one by one. It is sad to say that not everyone could receive this hospitality, although other families did try to help.

How to choose the young men was difficult. There was no favouritism, but my father, who was a senior officer and had experienced Burma as well as fighting in Malaya, thought he could spot the most traumatized. When he did, he spirited them away and handed them over to my mother, who would comfort and repair them as best she could. She was their healer.

During these same visits by the young soldiers, my older sister Jean would often ask me if I had awoken in the night and heard any talking or whispering. Sleeping the peace of the innocent, nothing ever woke me. What was this talking, this whispering? I was curious. On weekends I had occasionally seen my father out of uniform, white long-sleeved shirt and white trousers, pipe, lit or unlit, grasped gently in his hand, talking softly to one of our young and battered guests. There was a presence about the scene which told me instinctively that the peaceful moment was not to be disturbed, even by a curious young boy. It was all very quiet and caring with the occasional word being caught and carried on the breeze. There was calmness as I carried on my way around my home and gardens, exploring and using my imagination as young boys do.

These were the same conversations heard by my Sister during the night in quiet corners of the house or even in a guest bedroom if the dreams had been too dark for the occupants.

I have often described my father as the quietest and kindest man I have known, an interesting description for an honoured soldier who had seen and lived the worst, but whose life was the very antithesis of that harshness. It was in the whispered, caring, calming conversations that the young wounded lions in Malaya received the teachings to move forward. That was the role of the "Whisperer"; not thrust upon him, but gently offered with healing words and the experience earned in the worst and the best of a life well lived.

We are getting better at welcoming our traumatised military, opening our arms and shifting our uncomfortable feelings about how to be at one with them. We have a long way to go, but if we can reach out and look at the simplicity of the human acts of grace of the Healer and Whisperer and take those small steps, then we will shift the paradigm.

CHAPTER 7

AH KWAI AND THE COOKBOOK OF LIFE

My sister Jean is the most amazing cook. I have recognised this since my late teens, when food started to become something more than fuel defined by quantity. Cooking became intertwined with our sparse reunions.

During our one-on-one relationship we have usually been separated by thousands of miles, compounded by long years without seeing each other. Jean was almost nine and my brother eleven when I was born in the idyllic town (it still is) of Northallerton in North Yorkshire, England. Our longest continuous span together was in my first eleven years, which were spent in England and Malaya. Thereafter there are stories to tell.

In my eleventh year we were separated when I went to school in England. She lived her life in Malaysia and Singapore for the next 45 years before finally retiring to the home of her blood, the United Kingdom, with her husband. During her South East

Asian years she would return to England and Scotland every few years for lengthy restorative vacations and to rekindle the fire of family. I in turn have lived in England, Canada, the Caribbean and more recently, the USA. The ties that bind are strong, as are our memories, which we share in the comfort of each other's company when I fly to visit her. It was during her UK sojourns that we managed to catch up, to share and stitch the years together, as we have now become the elders in the family. Our patchwork quilt of life is whole again.

In those pauses when I stayed with Jean, meals were an important part of our routine, and they still are to this day. Even though she was out of the "entertaining mode" of her Asian life, our main meals were amazing, eclectic and yet seem simply prepared. When she asked "what would you like for dinner?", my response was never a statement of desire but one of supplication garnished with anticipation. Whatever came out of her kitchen to be served in her various dining rooms, which always seemed to overlook well-tended, brilliant gardens, was not only beautifully presented; each unto itself was a testament to a skilled chef who worked magic.

Jean was always prepared, and planning was a must. The closest towns, small and historic, were ten miles away from her home through rolling hills and valleys stitched by narrow, twisting roads. Cupboards and freezers had to be well stocked, especially in winter when snow and ice could close access for days on end.

Succulent fresh lamb, local vegetables, fresh salmon or trout were all available. Spices for soups, things Asian, had been collected for years, the cupboards a treasure trove of the world, and a variety of sauces were conjured up. The day after a comforting meal we may well move into the elegance of the French or the sauces of their neighbouring Italian chefs. And given her decades of Asian years some part of that would make an entrance to the elegant but simply set table with its window on her world.

Our mother was recognised as a good cook but really her repertoire was not that wide, as it had been suffocated by the food rationings that were in force in the first half of the twentieth century, buttressed by two world wars. But the comfort foods and smells still linger in memory so much that they almost become real. The smells of newly-baked bread and biscuits (cookies to the uninitiated) and freshly-baked fruit pies are still in the air. My father's garden, a place of solace for him, offered up apples, pears, gooseberries, rhubarb, blackberries, raspberries, the occasional crop of strawberries; what a delight. Creations appeared, freshly warmed, out of the simple oven and were occasionally accompanied with fresh cream. Ice cream, never; a fridge was not needed, a pantry was cool enough. And as if those delights were not enough there were always the decadent sponge cakes, soft, moist and garnished with creams and jam. The cake would cool and then be sliced into worthy pieces with the cream and jam layered in. I can see them, smell them and taste them still.

This past fall, autumn to many of us, I spent more comforting time with my dear sister in Scotland. Memories were rekindled and indulged, of pride in our opportunities and in our parents, our histories in different parts of the world and the love of those countries which forged us and left their mark. Always, always there was talk of the brother we lost too soon in the prime of life. On my last trip at the conclusion of yet another savoured meal, I said to Jean "You must have learned to cook when you were just a young girl with Maud [our mother's name, we often used the first names of our parents] because when we got to Malaya, Maud trained her own cooks." Jean's reply surprised me. "No,

Maud never let me into her kitchen, even as a young girl. It was her preserve, she had things to do, no children allowed!"

I was momentarily at a loss for words. "So how on earth did you learn, how can you cook these Italian, French, English, Asian meals, some of which I can even remember from my pre-teen years?" There was a short silence, a sigh. The quiet but firm answer came, "It was Ah Kwai. It was all Ah Kwai."

In the 1940s the island of Penang, known as the Pearl of the Orient, located off the north-west coast of the Malay peninsula, was a bustling, thriving, vibrant trading port, as it had been for centuries. It was the home of diversity, a cornucopia of races from all over the world and a mix of languages to compete with Babel. Businesses of every type flourished. There were restaurants in abundance, crafted goods, home industries, weaving, small agriculture, fishing and the bustle of a busy harbour on one of the key trade routes in Asia. Family dynasties were created and left their mark.

The European countries still had a presence. Among them was a French family with young children. They were well established in Penang in commerce, but also had had other duties with the French consulate. As with all expatriates, local staff were employed in their home and were key in keeping the home running and tending the welfare of the children. A special bond always seemed to develop between children and their carers, often closer than that of parents. My nieces relish the wonderful times they had with those that shared their household.

One such young lady was a beautiful Chinese girl, long black hair down to her lower back, surprisingly tall for a Chinese, taller even than the lady of the house. One could certainly see her head above the crowds when she walked, glided, through the busy, bustling throngs and the cacophony of life that surrounded the street life of Penang with its competing languages of Malay,

Indian, Chinese, English, French and a smattering of others all boldly shouted. This was Ah Kwai. She was the key in the French household. She had a gift of learning and her young mistress, trained in French cuisine, in turn shared her knowledge with her. That was supplemented by Ah Kwai being available to work in other households where English, Indian or a variety of Chinese/Asian dishes might have been the menus of choice. She learned, she excelled, and she was always in demand. If you could have Ah Kwai, then the household took on a different aura; it was if you were one of the chosen Mems (from the Indian 'Memsahib', a title of distinction).

But war, devastation, the misery and the bloodbath of hell was coming. The word "humane" would disappear from life. The Japanese Army with its accompanying atrocities was coming through the Malay peninsula, and the Europeans had to escape if possible; the British Army and its allies were defeated and subjugated. Ah Kwai, with her presence, had to be protected, as her life would have been a living hell; death would be better. It was decided that first her hair had to be cut, chopped off unevenly to disguise her beauty and more closely define her features to resemble a male. Her pyjama-style clothing, which still had a feminine touch, was passed off to others and she started to wear older, shabbier clothing, to give her a male appearance. Her companionship with other women dwindled as she spent more time with the men labouring. Her hands became roughened, as did her feet. Comfort, family, safety as she knew it were in the past. She left Penang and went to a small village on the mainland, where she faded into the background.

Whether nomadic or in a village, family groups could be made up of the cross-section of Malays, Indians and Chinese, all of course local. Food was hard to find for all on the peninsula. The coastal kampongs fared the best with their fishing enterprises, the inland villages less so. Ah Kwai toiled in the small rice fields and vegetable patches, subsistence living. Yams, guava, sweet potatoes and tapioca supplemented the meagre diets, as did the native coconuts. Food once again played a part in her life. Her adopted family got away in time and she moved around, partly nomadic, as some villages had to be on the move and start all over again. She kept a low profile, and was not singled out. The earthen floors were her bed. There was also a period when she was hidden as labourer on one of the many rubber plantations.

At the end of the war, Ah Kwai returned to Penang, to which her French "family" had also returned. But the world had changed and families began to be repatriated to their homelands, and so it was time for her adopted family to join the throng and return to the motherland, the France they had left so many years before. By that time my sister was in Penang with her own young family. She heard of Ah Kwai, now so much older, and instantly took a liking to her. Jean's understanding of her was underscored by knowledge of our own life in Malaya, shared with our father when he was part of a long offensive which saw the defeat of the communist insurgencies that had arisen. We shared that life and the Malaysian culture. Ah Kwai joined her new family, essentially to care for my sister's children, and that was when she decided to gradually start to share her own culinary gifts. She passed on what she had learned and mastered in her pre-war life. What a blessing for Jean!

Ah Kwai accompanied the family as the growth in business made Kuala Lumpur and Singapore home. My youngest niece was born in Singapore. Ah Kwai was devoted to the girls, who in her eyes were her very own. When the parents went out on an evening it was the signal for Ah Kwai to enter the girls' bedroom to care for them, smother them with love and protect them. As they fell asleep, she lay on the floor between them and lightly closed her eyes, but she would never totally sleep. She was not uncomfortable and had slept the same way for years on the earthen floors in villages and the jungle. When she sensed the car lights coming up the driveway, she would silently scurry back to her own room. It was a secret pact; the parents would never know. The girls were safe.

What she did not know was that when Jean and her husband returned home they would pull into the driveway, make sure the car lights were on high, and idle the engine for a moment before driving the car all the way in. This would give her time to scurry back to her own rooms and they would then see her shadowy movements. Then they would park the car and enter the house. Her secret was safe, in her mind, and her mission was fulfilled. As this procedure became routine, Jean began to place a comfortable mat and blankets under one of the girls' beds. Nothing was said to Ah Kwai, who had a secret pride, but those blankets were used every time the parents left the home.

Jean readily credits that beautiful Chinese woman for sharing her culinary skills. Ah Kwai retired before my sister returned to the UK and before that the children, young adults at university, had also left their Asian homes. The Ah Kwais of the world were able to retire in some comfort. They had been well paid and had never had any overhead expenses, and most families where employment had been long-term would also provide a lump payment or pension for the people who had been such an integral part of their family life. The Ah Kwais of the world were family. In many cases the elders would return to their home villages, or as was the custom of many, be taken in by their children. Ah Kwai still lingers in memory and no doubt is a silent guest in the dining room when certain meals are enjoyed and her name bubbles through.

CHAPTER 8

THE BLACK ROLLS ROYCE

Lady Isabel Gurney, wife of Sir Henry Gurney, the British High Commissioner to the Federation of Malaya (pre-Malaysia), had visited our home at The Big House in Port Dickson on a few occasions. The visits were essentially her part in waving the flag and providing support to the families of British officers living some eight thousand miles from their homeland; close to four weeks by sea away in those days. She was a generous, boisterous yet warm person who took a personal interest in the lives of those she met. Where she could get away with it, she did not hide behind the curtain of pomp and circumstance.

Our home was chosen because it was the largest available for such occasions, and with its lush gardens and sweeping driveway it was fitting for the responsibility of hosting the British Government's Representative, with all the surface protocol that entailed. The black Rolls Royce, flag flying, would sweep up the driveway, usually chaperoned by a couple of jungle-green military Land Rovers and the requisite black police car. Local dignitaries, merchants and the military cohort were all present. My mother was an amazing organiser and blessed with a wonderful and dedicated staff, most of whom lived on the premises, and she always drew the short straw. At the end of the day the black Rolls Royce would leave with its emissary intact and we would all be treated to a regal wave as it made its way down the driveway.

It was not long after one of these visits that we saw Lady Isabel in a more formal setting. She would have come across many seven-year-old boys during her role as the High Commissioner's wife, yet it was no surprise when she singled me out, on 21 February 1951, at a ceremony in Government House in Kuala Lumpur, the capital. Government House was one of those many magnificent white civic colonial buildings, in the French Renaissance style, built by the British across their Empire in the late eighteenth and through to the early twentieth century. It still stands today among many other white buildings of inspiring beauty. White seemed to be the colour of that time. I was turned out smartly in my new white shirt and shorts, specially made by my father's tailor. My sister tells me that Lady Gurney's remarks to me were along the lines of "How nice to see you again. I think you are the youngest invited guest we have ever had at Government House. And you are dressed so smartly and have been very well behaved." All very British!

Sir Henry Gurney had just awarded my father, turned out in full white dress military uniform, sword sheathed, the military honour of the MBE (Member of the Order of The British Empire) in recognition of his services in Malaya. An option was to be invested in this Order at Buckingham Palace at some later date; my father deferred, as he believed that this recognition was equally for his staff, Malay and British.

The British were not doing too well in the post-war battle against the Communist Terrorists in Malaya at this time. In the late 1940s, a counter-insurgency unit known as Force Ferret was formed by the British and Malayan authorities as part of their response to the communist insurgency. This was the start-up model to help establish doctrine for British operations in the jungle; it was unique. My father had been singled out for this operation by the same Field Marshall who had promoted him in Burma, Field Marshall Slim.

Part of the medal citation reads: "Although Lt Gill took over his duties on 12 July 1948, over 200 men were fully equipped and armed for prolonged jungle operations, [and] had been deployed in their theatre of operations by the end of that month. Later the force increased to over 600 units, all ranks. He has often cheerfully worked until the early hours of the morning forgoing all leisure and personal comfort. His example of devotion has earned for him the respect and affection of all races in the force, and has had a direct effect in inspiring a high state of morale." That was the father I knew.

That event was our last meeting with Lady Gurney. Eight months later, on October 6, 1951, Sir Henry was assassinated. On their way to Fraser's Hill in the Cameron Highlands, the Gurneys were in their black Rolls Royce, familiar to us, with a driver and their Secretary and were accompanied by some military personnel in a Land Rover and armed Scout Car. They were ambushed by Communist Terrorists. The spraying automatic fire killed the driver immediately. Sir Henry pushed his wife and her Secretary to the floor of the car. Bullets kept coming. He then opened the car door, got out, slammed it shut and ran away from the car as far as he could. He was cut down in a hail of bullets and after a while the shots were silenced. Lady Gurney and the Secretary got out of the car unharmed; the terrorists had withdrawn. They found Sir Henry's bullet-ridden body in a ditch. He had achieved what he had set out to do; he had saved his wife and her Secretary by drawing away the stream of bullets. He was only 53.

That ambush escalated military action with over 1500 British, Gurkha and Malayan troops being deployed in the jungle, supported by strafing and bombing by the British and Australian air forces.

Sir Henry was buried with dignity in Kuala Lumpur and it was significant that the funeral was heavily attended by Malayan people of all backgrounds and from all levels of society. He was acknowledged for the leadership he had brought to Malaya in those difficult times and for the personal bravery he had shown.

Our own lives didn't change too much, although we now had a greater presence of armed Malay Regiment personal visible around our homes, in the towns and markets, but generally we were safe.

Fast forward some sixty-plus years. In 2014, 63 years after the above events, I returned to Malaysia. A walk through Kuala Lumpur brought into focus the old white colonial buildings where I had last seen the Gurneys. In both Kuala Lumpur and the island of Penang there were many roads and modern plazas bearing the name of Gurney; people were still appreciative of his efforts in the eventual formation of their country. Finally in Penang, strolling through the bustling old streets of disparate cultures, again inhaling the smells of the sea, scents of foods and fragrances from across Asia, my wife and I stopped suddenly outside a government building. There on display, still polished and cared for, was the old black Rolls Royce, bullet holes showing. It was the very same car that had climbed the long driveway to The Big House in Port Dickson so many years ago, linking the past and the present.

CHAPTER 9

A FEW SLEEPLESS NIGHTS

Port Dickson, Malaya 12 July 1948-26 Sept 1948

Copy of the original transcript in the UK national archives. Charles Gill was awarded the MBE by Sir Henry Gurney, High Commissioner of Malaya, Representative of King George VI:

Lieut (QM*) C. Gill was appointed as QM Force Ferret immediately following his arrival in Malaya from the United Kingdom. It was essential that this mixed force of civilians and military personnel, comprising five different nationalities, should be equipped and in the field in the shortest possible time. To assist him Lt. Gill had a very small staff of mixed nationality, hastily collected, and in many cases untrained, and which had not fully assembled before Lt Gill took over his duties.

Due to a shortage of trained staff, Lt Gill had to personally prepare all indents, check and record all stores, equipment and clothing received and issued. In addition he had to supervise the collection and issue of rations, and supervise the building of temporary accommodation. This work also entailed the meetings of trains at Seremban, thirty miles away, on an average of four times a week, to take consignments of stores, etc.

Although Lt Gill took over his duties on 12th July 1948, over 200 men, fully equipped and armed for prolonged jungle operations, had been deployed in their theatre by the end of the third month. Later the force increased to over 600 all ranks.

Lt Gill has shown a very high sense of responsibility as well as determination and initiative in overcoming all the many difficulties which have arisen in the administration of a force of this nature. He has often cheerfully worked until the early hours of the morning forgoing all leisure and personal comfort. His example of devotion to duty has earned for him the support and affection of all races in the force, and has had a direct effect in inspiring a high state of morale.

*QM: Quarter Master

CHAPTER 10

THE QUIET GARDENER

The old soldier was a quiet man; quiet in demeanour, conversation and the appreciation of the world, his family, his life. The military accolades from a grateful country for service given in lands far away were unobtrusive in the quiet darkness of a desk drawer. He had found a well-deserved peace. Perhaps his quietness was his strength in overcoming man's inhumanity to man. He was respected in his world journeys and trusted by those whom his life had touched in his home country and far away Asiatic lands.

He was a small framed man; his first induction letter into military service showed him at five feet seven inches and weighing less than 120 pounds. His body curved in later life, but was still dignified and gave the illusion of a strength of spirit and crispness of military precision. His hair was sparse and silver compared to his original dark blond. Not a prideful man, he did nevertheless take delight that his original hair colour was inherited from the Viking and Nordic tribes that had invaded his country some fifteen hundred years ago and his Roman nose a tribute to the legions which had also inhabited this land and left their defining marks. A noble heritage indeed.

Where does one find peace, solace, the place where nothing intrudes to disturb tranquillity or the time to reflect, the place where one can absorb the life-giving breath of nature, life itself? Peace, calm, unfolding wonders that can still stimulate the senses, the competing soft smells of freshness, the rustles of small creatures in the undergrowth and the trilling songs of birds at dawn and dusk. The myriad colours that outnumber the colours of the short-lived rainbows, the textures of leaves, petals and stems are never static; osmosis is forever.

Our quiet gardener knew within his soul that this bountiful gift was not free. There is a worthy nurturing role one must play in becoming the protector and cultivator. You must tend your Eden with care, appreciation and humility. You share of yourself, you are part of the bigger picture; all life has its seasons.

I knew this man, still do, who found such a place, his paradise, his oasis, his refuge. The small garden he could see from his kitchen window stretched before him for some sixty yards and was perhaps twenty yards wide at the most. It was his part of his homeland in north-east England, close to the town of his birth. He would gaze over this on a morning as he prepared a freshly-brewed tea for his wife of some forty-plus years.

His eyes would focus first on his beloved rose bushes, no matter what the season. They were examined daily and fed, with little adjustments here and there. And when in bloom, their heads and blossoms were tenderly touched. The blooms were magnificent, a myriad of colours. Their caregiver was in his element; he received such joy and knew in turn that pleasure was given to others who could see these magnificent flowers. He had tried many times, for years, to cultivate a black rose. That was forever elusive to him, yet he knew within himself that someday, not in his time perhaps, that variety would appear, and it did.

Beyond the rose garden there was a small square of well-tended grass, where the white terrier who was his companion would lie. A glance away and the lawn was fringed on two sides by flower beds with flowers of the season and at the outer edge, just by the old greenhouse, was a small rockery which was allowed to grow wild. The greenhouse was home to seedlings which would later be transplanted in the garden beyond. It was also host to tomatoes of a few varieties, and these were the first fruits to come to the table.

Moving beyond the greenhouse, our gardener had an array of fruits and vegetables. His wife was never short of nourishing flavours to make her enticing fruit pies. Vegetables in abundance graced the main course meals. The rows were neat and orderly in the earlier years. The offerings of this land of plenty were gooseberries, rhubarb, raspberries, blackberries and occasionally strawberries. The fruits shared the garden with health-giving vegetables strung out over all the seasons in the year. Peas, string beans, carrots, cabbage, lettuce, cauliflowers and Brussels sprouts. Potatoes were not needed, as they were provided by a farm only minutes away.

The king of the fruits was the apple, and these grew on three trees. They were picked fresh and sparingly. At the end of the season, what remained of the small crop would be wrapped in newspaper and held in the attic to be enjoyed throughout the winter. Picking a fresh apple every day possible was ingrained in our gardener's habits.

I can see him on a morning in an open-necked shirt, pipe lit, the aroma of Player's Cut Golden Bar tobacco wafting and curling in the breeze, slowly tying the laces of his old hand-crafted army boots, clean as usual, then slowly making his way down the narrow walkway. A pause perhaps at the rows of his crops, a tamping of the pipe tobacco, a slow inhale and then the comfort showed on his face as the old pipe did its work and created familiar feelings of well-being. Partway through the morning there would be the reward of an apple gently plucked and then polished on his trousers. He would sit on a stool or a step and softly peel it with his penknife, the peel always coming away in one piece. The apple was sliced delicately and slowly, and only when one slice was eaten would another be carved.

Those were halcyon days for our quiet gardener. The numbered days were not as many as his devotion and sacrifice to his country, but the goodness of nature was a soothing force that took away the past and let the gardener know that his hands were needed in the new growth of the cycle of life.

As the years passed it seemed that the garden grew even larger and the spirit was vibrant, but the tiring body could not keep up. The land beyond the greenhouse gradually returned to fallow land but was kept tidy by some help from the nearby farm. The quiet gardener saved his energy for the small lawn and the immediate rose garden close to the house. The roses continued to bloom, well-tended, and gave comfort. The occasional walk was taken down the garden path, the pipe inhaled.

Spring came early one year and the roses bursting in all their glory were at their best one April morning, each colour magnified and glistening. It was the day when those old but clean army boots were left by the backdoor, their final march behind them, and no soft streams of tobacco scents were woven in the garden. The quiet gardener, the old soldier, had taken his last walk in his Eden.

Some thirty years after the last walk into the garden by our quiet gardener, I visited his paradise. I introduced myself to new owners and was given a warm welcome and a tour of the garden with which I was so familiar. They had such pride in it, especially in their roses, which were still admired by those who lived on the long, winding country lane. There had been change, but not to those still incredible roses in full bloom. I saw them as they always had been, miraculous in their colours and posture. Perhaps they were tended by some unseen, gently nurturing guiding hand while the other hand held on to a well-worn pipe. Did some rose have a different scent or was that a hint of pipe smoke I sensed between the stems?

Charles Gill WW2, Asia

Charles Gill WW2, Asia

Charles Gill WW2, Asia

Charles Gill WW2, UK

Granny Gill and Jean

Maud, Charles and Granny Gill

Wedding Charles and Maud

Edward, Arthur and Charles

Granny Gill and Alan

Jean and Gerald

Gerald, Jean and Alan   Maud, Jean and Alan

Gerald and Jean

Charles and Edward

Gerald

Charles

HMT Empire Windrush

Alan

Charles Gill and Fellow Officer

Maud and Charles

Singapore Arrival

Northallerton; All Saints Church

Northallerton; Porch House

Northallerton; High Street

Northallerton; Thomson Butchers

Northallerton; Aerial View

CHAPTER 11

"BE OFF WITH THE OLD LOVE BEFORE YOU ARE ON WITH THE NEW"

A century before the birth of Christ the Roman dramatist Plautus wrote in his comedy Trinummus: "He who plunges into love is more lost than if he leapt from a rock!" Or as Plautus, Chaucer and Shakespeare said over and over again, "if you love her you cannot see her, because love is blind."

How many of us have been blinded? But while these adages hold some truth there is none more poignant than mother's warning of "be off with the old love before you are on with the new". A mother's advice can often seem cold, but was meant kindly. In my youth – when was that again? – there were no warm talks. We were after all parent and child. We loved unconditionally but had a shroud of "let's not talk of it". Now in my later decades I can look back and see the warning and portents of the stirring storm to follow.

Mother's caution was directed to my older-by-a-decade brother, Jim for short. He rode the waves of passion before me and in a way smoothed the seas to be explored. Though stricken and lamed by polio, he was a stocky, handsome swarthy young man with charisma, charm and intellect, and was a gifted surgeon. He was also a breaker of hearts. How often I had heard our mother gently admonish him. Yet she was gracious, as was my father, and the exquisite, to me smouldering, women he brought to our home were always welcome. My parents were cautious enough never to get names mixed. But he was loved unconditionally and through all the physical and emotional pain, he left in his wake a trail of broken hearts. And yet those links remained strong in later years.

He was, is, my yardstick, my role model. The sixties were upon us. Swinging England was upon us. Indulgence, the peace of the Ban the Bomb marches, the angst of Vietnam. And the exploding music and the new rebellious mantra of "sex, drugs and rock and roll." I was a child of the new world with a periphery vision of the old. My father's way of devotion to family, God, King and country was admired but fading. It was time to ride the magic bus.

Following my schooling, for which I am ever grateful, and especially for the patience of those great teachers that unleashed our minds, I immediately moved away from home to another city and my first full-time employment in my first profession of banking. I still remained in northern England this time, in the city of Leeds. I was at last free from the rigour (yet the best years of early life) of boarding school and its demand for academic and physical excellence. I left behind the contradictory mantras of "be a team player" and "be the leader, the alpha."

My new home was in a large three-storey terraced house with six other young men. Some were starting careers like me; others were postgraduate and PhD students. Our boarding house was our home for five days a week. Our gracious, proud, strict, caring and redoubtable but kindly host was Miss Scott, the owner. I still have the pewter beer mug engraved for my twenty-first birthday with those names that bring back good memories; Miss Scoot, Peter, Alan, John, Keith, Tom and Henry. None of us ever missed our evening dinner. Not only would we be gently scolded, but we would have missed the wonderful food that fuelled us. Miss Scott spoiled her young men. The cooking was amazing, the quantities were even better. No guests, no young ladies allowed. She was our protector.

My new freedom was having my own money, a starting wage, local and ancient pubs, active sports mid-week and weekends, good companionship, camaraderie through sports clubs and an eclectic group of friends. And away from home there was a whole new world of women, at work, out on an evening, as guests of other friends, the whole social scene and to top it all off it was the sixties! The future was distant; today was to be lived to its fullest. We were sailing on the wings of new freedoms, uncharted waters for most, a route directed by the background of Dylan, the Stones, the Beatles, and our most common drug of choice was alcohol. It crossed all barriers. Marijuana drifted only in the right atmosphere, behind closed doors, and, it often seemed, in dim light. Fun was innocent, bungling, naïve; dalliances became friendships and the oyster gradually opened. Friends became secure friends and something more.

There were escapes and laughter. Leeds was an old city and still had some of the old-time music halls going, some dating back to the late 1700s. In our era there were escape artists, dancers, music hall stars, comedy and tantalizing strip shows. Once a month we lads would go down; Thursday night was strip night. Most of the ladies were beyond their seductive prime but would tease as they demurely stripped to the pulsating beat of male hormonal laughter. We would sit within peanut-flipping distance. The artisans pursued their crafts and we ours. The objective was to pitch as many peanuts as possible into the fleshy folds of the breasts as they escaped their minimal covering. Thank god for ample flesh, for without it we would have been miserable failures. Our accolade was "Good shot, Henry", the quietest lad amongst us, and the ladies of temptation would complete their pantomime of gloves off, bustier off, and the revelation of cleavage, breasts and peanuts, all carefully sheltered by a large feathered fan which miraculously appeared. As we said, good clean fun.

And then I met Andrea – a thunderbolt. She was a beautiful woman with soft white English skin. Tall, my height, a great figure, she was a lady who moved with ease, conscious and confident of her appeal. Blonde hair, blue eyes flashing, always alive, alluring. Her eyes and mouth were always on the side of light, no darkness here. She was good for me. She laughed, her eyes laughed. She showed me tenderness, a coyness and loyalty. She rolled into my way of life, my pursuit of sports, yet did not take my freedom. I was a bachelor, no ties. We dated, we cared, we fell in love.

We shared our evenings when we could; she never got to Miss Scott's. We respected each other's commitments and she shared her family on weekends as a stop gap between my sports activities. She joined me in in my endeavours, ever encouraging. She was learning to play the guitar. She was a good, fair-minded, sensual and sexual woman who turned heads. She was quietly exciting. That was a golden year, a summer to be remembered. Sparkling eyes, trilling laughter, carefree days of friendships, sports; we lived in the moment. She showed me that sex could be love and love in itself could be complete without sex. She shared her grace, her tenderness, her passion and her appetites. And yet she loved me in a pure way that demanded no possession.

I was growing closer to this lady, so close that I knew I could spend my days with her. We talked of that; we were serious. And then my job demanded that I move away. I did, leaving her behind. Keeping in touch required commitment, which without phones, email and cars was not quite as easy as today. We continued to date. I travelled on Friday nights by train and returned to my new base, where my parents lived, late on a Sunday. Andrea, when possible, also took the journey to me. Mother loved the girl; her sincerity, her unassuming ways, her infectious glow. Dad was quieter and let us be. She was loved for who she was, and I was getting closer.

Then life intervened, punctuated by our absences. There were less frequent visits, fewer letters. I pursued sports on my home ground rather than travelling, and new friendships developed. To this day I am not sure how the relationship ended. I remember a letter from her father saying he was writing as she was in hospital for an eye operation. He was her scribe and he wrote as she dictated. All she wanted was an explanation of what had happened. She did not condemn or judge, she was too great a love for that.

I never saw her again except for once many, many years later. I was walking along a station platform in England. I glanced in the window of one coach and there she was, a silhouette of ethereal beauty, blonde hair pinned up, calmly staring into space, at peace; I could sense those blue eyes. Perhaps she had thoughts of other train journeys taken long ago. Did one of us make one too few? Had she sensed me, had she seen me? That vision gripped me and I see her still. Oh Andrea!

"Be off with the old love before you are on with the new," mother intoned in her own wisdom, as she knew I had not completed my passage with Andrea. And so a new lady moved into my life. She proved to be an incredible mother to our children, a good friend and loyal beyond belief. But Andrea had struck first, and she haunts me to this day.

How many of us go through that process until we finally end up with a new mate? If we had the wisdom to listen to mother, we would be more complete. We can't go back. We can imagine with our "what ifs", but it is better for our soul and mind to acknowledge what was, acknowledge our actions and acknowledge what is.

No matter how we flesh it out, a choice was made. How great it would have been to act on Mother's wisdom.

And so the years pass; I have not seen the mother of my children for some twenty years. Other storms raged, and life is what it is. Perhaps what I had in my grasp and let slip put an unknown shadow on any future relationship.

A few years ago, I was out for dinner with my daughter, who was in her thirties at the time. There is not much we do not share. It was a good evening. We started talking about family names and histories. It was then that my daughter said to me, "Dad, is it true you named me after an old girlfriend?" My reply was "Whoever told you that, Andrea?" Her answer "Mom!" She then asked me to tell her about my earlier life and about Andrea.

Life!

CHAPTER 12

THE DESERT'S MUSE: GERTRUDE BELL

Periods of time are often linked by the thinnest threads of fate. Such is the case with the lady in whom I have taken a great interest, and indeed who has captivated me. In our early years we shared the same home, although not at the same time, and both of us travelled through the Middle East and saw the warring events there. Our journeys have spanned some one hundred and fifty years.

In the late 1940s through to the early sixties, my brother and I, separated by some eleven years, were boarders at an old English Grammar School, Sir William Turner's in Redcar, North Yorkshire, England. The school had its roots in the sixteen hundreds through the auspices of the Lord Mayor of London, Sir William Turner.

As boarders we lived in a stately home, Red Barns, built in the late 1860s by Sir Hugh Bell, a local industrialist whose fortune rested on his significant ownership of railways, coal, iron and steel mills and the burgeoning might of the chemical industry. Hugh Bell was the son of Sir Isaac Bell, in turn one of the greatest industrialists in Europe, whose fortune has been put on a par with today's Bill Gates.

It was a magnificent house, not too ostentatious, as with the inherited aristocratic wealthy of the country. It had large rooms and ceilings, corridors and stairs in abundance and with windows on all sides, except those facing the street, and it was pleasantly lit and not dark and foreboding. It was functional, and surrounded on three sides by a large garden and stables. Its additional defining piece of richness was its own private railway siding, which allowed the private coaches of the Bells to pull in against the garden walkway.

Sir Hugh Bell was widowed and had been left with two young children. Society congregated around him. He was not an ostentatious person compared to most, and after a brief spell of mourning, all according to the dictates of the Victorian era, he married Florence Olliffe, a writer who was well known in the corridors of society and well versed in its suffocating etiquette. It was this lady who would become the stepmother to Gertrude Bell, Hugh's daughter. It was not an easy relationship for either woman, as Gertrude, still only a child, certainly marched to her own drummer.

Gertrude shrugged off the expected full immersion into the life of a young lady of society, but was wise enough to know she always had entry into the "who's who" of that society, those who held the power. Her grandfather and father were powerful figures, not by inherited riches and birth but by their own significant and industrious endeavours. Gertrude learned to hold and play the cards she had been dealt and, was not afraid to use them.

Gertrude Bell went to Oxford University; she was the first woman to obtain a first-class honours degree in History, which she achieved in two years. She also earned a reputation for challenging the status quo, being argumentative and very vocal. Women were not expected to speak in class. Her first love was languages, which were cultivated throughout her worldly travels, essentially to the Middle East, where she learned to be fluent in Arabic, Turkish and Persian. These were framed by her command of the more traditional European languages of French, German and Italian. She was also acknowledged as one of the leading mountaineers in Europe, male or female.

Bell was able to pursue her passions for archaeology, photography (in its infancy), world travels in Europe, the Middle East, her greatest love, and especially the desert with its diversified peoples of different religions, religions within religions, cultures and lineages going back thousands of years.

Gertrude's foray into the male dominated world of the Middle East was unprecedented. She was welcomed and admired by kings, princes and tribal leaders, especially when no public ear was given to the voices of their own women. In her travels she lived the life of the nomads, with her own camel, horse, tent, bed, desks and travelling trunks full of the necessities of life. That the men courted her views, confided in her, welcomed her into their families, religions and traditions is remarkable. Her writings reveal the intimacy of these meetings and indeed the insight into their personal family lives.

On many occasions she was the de-facto leader of British Middle East delegations. She had an official title, Oriental Secretary. She worked with Sir Winston Churchill and the legendary Colonel T. E. Lawrence, Lawrence of Arabia. Mighty company indeed! She forged the boundaries of the Arab States which became countries, and had a greater understanding of the Middle East than most of the politicians. Lawrence was the only one who was perhaps her equal; they worked in tandem. He had an identical degree to Bell from the same college, spoke fluent Arabic and some dialects, and was well connected to people in power whom he, like Bell, would use to meet his needs. To an extent they were "king-makers".

Gertrude Bell is inexorably linked to the history of the whole Middle East in the late nineteenth century and the first two decades of the twentieth. The Ottoman Empire, Iraq, Jordan, Palestine, all bear her footprint, and there is no doubt that even after her death in 1926 her opinions on the Zionist push for its own state, to which she was opposed, would still have carried weight.

She would however have felt her greatest achievement was being considered as one of the leading archaeologists in the whole region. Her phenomenal leadership, knowledge, ability to get things done is acknowledged by many countries; the Iraqi Museum has a wing named after her.

Gertrude, or Gertie, as she was affectionately known by us schoolboys who inhabited her home, was a mythical figure. We knew of her, that she had walked our corridors, perhaps still did, but didn't know the heights of her influence in the world. As we pursued our studies of the arts, languages, mathematics, sciences, the history that was England and thus the world, excellence in sports, missing in our curriculum was the history of Gertrude Bell. Her particular era was not part of our focus, and so it is in these later years we can search for what we missed and have her own research and writings available to inspire us.

Gertrude Bell died in July 1926 in Baghdad.

RECOMMENDED BOOKS

The Desert and the Sown, Travels in Palestine and India,
Gertrude Bell

Gertrude Bell, Queen of the Desert, Shaper of Nations,
Georgina Howell

The latter book contains indices showing Gertrude Bell's published letters, work, and books, some in the public domain, others not.

Faisal Ibn Hussein, King of Iraq, first met Gertrude Bell following an introduction by T.E. Lawrence (Lawrence of Arabia). Following Faisal's coronation he invited her to the first dinner party at his house; she was treated as a queen, both during her journey and on arrival. To meet Faisal on this occasion Gertrude was taken up the ancient Tigris River in his launch. She wrote to him:

"Have I ever told you what the river is like on a hot summer night? At dusk the mist hangs in long white bands over the water; the twilight fades and the lights of the town shine out on either bank, with the river, dark and smooth and full of mysterious reflections, like a road of triumph through the mist. Silently a boat with a winking headlight slips down the stream, then a company of quffahs, each with his tiny lamp, loaded to the brim with watermelons from Samarra... And we slow down the launch so that the wash may not disturb them. The waves of our passage don't even extinguish the floating votive candles each burning on its minute boat made out of the swathe of a date cluster, with anxious hands launched above the town – if they reach the last town yet burning, the sick man will recover, the baby will be born safely into this world of hot darkness and glittering lights... Now I've brought you out to where the palm trees stand marshalled along the banks. The water is so still you can see the Scorpion on it, star by star... and here are Faisal's steps".

From Gertrude Bell, Queen of Nations.

CHAPTER 13

Kathleen Brown: she shouted and the world heard her

As a boy in my early teenage years I spent several weeks of the summer with my sister Jean in small towns such as Cookham Dean and Maidenhead by the meandering River Thames in the south of England. They were idyllic times. It was there that I met Kathleen Fraser, more famously known as Kathleen Brown. Kathleen was Jean's mother-in-law.

Kathleen was a diminutive woman with extremely long hair, and was close to seventy at the time. There was power in her eyes and in her bearing; it seemed she would not suffer fools gladly. I was certainly not familiar with older people, who looked askance at young boys, and I regret now that I could not engage Kathleen and her husband Donald more. Theirs is a history of colonial lives lived in India and Africa, service to country with the Indian Civil Service and the British Service, farms bought and lost. My brother-in-law, Darien, and one of his sisters were born in Mombasa, on Kenya's east coast along the great Indian Ocean, during part of this journey.

What I did learn at that point was that Kathleen had been a Suffragette, one of those strong women from all levels of society who fought the Government and the status quo, broke laws, suffered harsh punishment, took to violence and finally won. They did not seek to glorify themselves. It was a fight not just for the right to vote but for the rights of equality. The family lore, or story, at the time was that Kathleen was one of those who chained themselves to the railings of 10 Downing Street, the Prime Minister's Official Residence, and for their troubles were jailed for seven days. It was pay the fine or prison. The fines went unpaid.

It was a time of violence, anger, vicious struggles and punishments meted out harshly and savagely. These women were militants; they were in a war and fought aggressively for their cause. Their motto was "Deeds Not Words". Laws would be broken. There were protests in Parliament, in the streets and in all corners of England. The leadership did not quake. Emmeline Pankhurst was arrested for brawling. She faced six weeks in prison, in solitary confinement in a stone-cold cell.

Age was not a barrier. In 1905 Emily Davies, who had qualified with a Doctorate in Law at 71, was one of those handing a petition to the Prime Minister. Emily Pankhurst was approaching her fifties and a sixty-year-old widow led the crusade on another deputation.

Although born in the north of England in a small town called Ryton, close to Newcastle, Kathleen's efforts covered all areas of England and her contributions were governed by what some call "northern grit". Nothing was too much, and you fought on regardless. There was only one result that was acceptable: win, and win at all costs if necessary.

Kathleen Brown was in good company. The Houses of Parliament were under attack by one group of women, but they were broken up by the police. This group of over one hundred were charged with assaulting police, damaging property and so on. It was a violent confrontation. However, in all the chaos the prosecution could not truly identify the prisoners, so the trial was adjourned. At this same time Kathleen and accomplices were charged with stone throwing, and they were all sentenced to solitary confinement in Holloway prison. All the suffragettes went on a hunger strike for seven days. They were released after that time, without having broken their fast. Immediately on release some of the suffragettes went on to another part of the country, Birmingham, and continued their cycle of disruption, arrest, hunger strikes, release. The dark side then took over and the force feeding of women became common – an outrageous and terrifying assault. None of this appeared to make any difference to the parliamentarians, who continued with their meaningless and demeaning speeches.

Further north, near Doncaster in South Yorkshire (north central England), Kathleen Brown was at work. She was part of a group planning to attack Wheatley Hall. This old stately home had been built in the 1680s by rich landowners and was surrounded by vast natural parklands. It was thought that its destruction or significant damage would be a blow to the elite landowners. However, it was not to be, and Kathleen and her group in the safe house disbanded and went onto other more viable options.

In 1909, the Prime Minister, Lloyd George, made his way to Newcastle in the North of England, where he was to speak at a meeting in an area of the town known as The Haymarket. Significantly all tickets were marked "Not to be sold to a Woman." As expected the event was ripe for protest and additional police had been called in from the capital, London. The women were at their active best that night. A report headed "Mapping Radical Tyneside" stated:

- Winnifred Jones broke a window in the door of the Palace Theatre

- Lady Constance and Emily Wilding Davison stood outside the Newcastle Brewery Offices in the Haymarket. Lady Litton threw a stone at Sir Walter Runciman's car. Emily Wilding Davison was arrested by a plain clothes policeman as she took a stone from her pocket.

- Jane Brailsford took an axe from a bunch of flowers and attacked the barriers.

- Miss Pitman broke a window in the Barass Bridge Post Office.

- Miss Kathleen Brown broke a window in the Pink Lane Post Office.

Kathleen Brown continued her activism. She was imprisoned three times. Following one of her convictions, when she was sentenced to seven days' solitary confinement in Holloway Prison, she returned to Newcastle and her northern roots. She was met in that July of 1909 by large crowds of supporters at Newcastle Central Station. There were great festivities, with colourful banners and flags, and cars and coaches covered with coloured ribbons and flowers. The Suffragette colours of green, purple and white were to be seen everywhere. Kathleen was escorted to the Turk's Head Hotel for a celebration and the opportunity to talk to the large crowds that had followed the procession. The momentum has never stopped.

There is an anecdote about Kathleen from one of the prison diaries of an 'Unknown Suffragette'. On Tuesday July 13, 1909, Prisoner DX322 (presumed to be 18-year-old Gladys Roberts) wrote:

"I heard the bell at a quarter to six and got up after a very good night. The wardress came just after I was dressed. I washed in my pail as best I could and she said "Will you empty your slops please?" which I did. I then rolled up my bed and made the cell tidy, all the time having conversations with Miss Spring in the adjoining cell. I can't make Kathleen Brown hear". That was the end of that entry,

"I can't make Kathleen Brown hear." Well, the world certainly heard from Kathleen Brown. But what Gladys Roberts did not know about that diminutive powerhouse for change Kathleen Brown was that she was deaf. That had never been a barrier to change.

The Representation of People Act was finally passed into law in 1918. The Act was so-named as prior to this as all non-householders were precluded from voting, not just women.

CHAPTER 14

THE SPY WHO
LOVES ME (STILL)

*(With apologies to the iconic creations of
James Bond and George Smiley whom we owe to
Ian Fleming and John Le Carré)*

The Malaya of the 1940s and 1950s was the very antithesis of Pandora's Box in that while it released the gifts and magic of Malaya to me, there was no evil, only mystery and hope. The mystery was the unfolding of life itself. Nothing was ever like it, and in its haunting it has continued to cast its spell on me to this very day. It was as if a living canvas of one of the great masters had sprung to life and offered me a whole new world. This world was South East Asia with its beauty and its promise of ever-unfolding mysteries, a life to be experienced and absorbed with joy and eternal gratitude. The viciousness and decimation of World War Two was left behind; the mixed populace of Malay, British, Chinese, East Indian, Tamil and others were working together, trusting and not, to create a new world, with the shackles of colonialism sprung open, a dream of hope to be admired. This was my playground as a young boy.

The economy of Malaya was almost non-existent. The rich tin mines and the rubber plantations which had changed the world by feeding its industrialisation had ground to a halt. The economy was broken, raped and pillaged by the demands of warring nations. The Big War might have been over, but the war for the country, its sultanates and dreams of independence and the minds and hopes of the people was not.

The British, returning after their humiliating retreat to Singapore, were the major cog in a coalition of military that included newly-formed regiments, Malay, Gurkha, various British regiments and the Australian Air Force. The police, while their ties with the military operations were blurred, also played a significant part in these wars. The roles of the police and military were different, ostensibly one military and one civilian yet interwoven like the writhing creeping jungle foliage, but it was essential that intelligence and planning was shared to ensure success. Opposing the march forward was the Malay Communist Party, adept at jungle warfare, propaganda, sabotage of roads and telephone lines, tortuous action against kampongs and villagers; in all, a force to be reckoned with.

Plans, information, strategy, timelines, troops and equipment required, communications, casualty expectations (enemy and civilian) and all the other ingredients of warfare had to be communicated in this jungle warfare. How could this be done without alerting the enemy, the MCP (Malay Communist Party) which was so well versed in jungle warfare and hit and run skirmishes? While the MCP had some very strong women who were also leaders, it was generally accepted that the civilian female population, as well as children, were off limits to the warring factions. I say generally, but not always.

This was understood in the small west coastal town of Port Dickson midway down the peninsula, where it was rumoured that even some of the communist leaders took a rest. These were interesting times in which to grow up. I knew nothing of the war except for the changing mood and silence when a soldier or police officer was killed and a family, with possibly one of my friends, now fatherless, had to move back to England. I was the perfect innocent foil. Children and women would not be harmed. It was only in much later years that I learned I had played an unwitting role in some of the messaging of planned jungle warfare and the march to freedom and independence.

My sister Jean, at 17 more than eight years older than me, worked in a secretarial position in the Regimental Adjutant's office; that role required her to sign the British Official Secrets Act. Like many who had signed the Act, she took great joy and relish in later years when asked about her role during those times of conflict by answering "if I told you, then I would have to kill you!" This is the same Act signed some years earlier in the Second World War by those magnificent women in Bletchley who deciphered the Enigma Code, hastening the end of the Axis supremacy in naval warfare. Who could predict that some fifty-plus years later, one of these ladies would be a neighbour of my sister in the Scottish Borders and a member of the same bridge club? A small world indeed.

There were very few strikingly beautiful, young, eligible and educated European women gracing the social calendar of Malay Society in the mid-twentieth century. Jean was an exception. Even more rare were potential male suitors who were not part of the military. It would have been very difficult for any aspiring lovers to meet; there was little space except their own homes, with parents or servants present, military venues, or perhaps a club at the racetrack. Nothing would be private.

This was fertile ground on which to hatch a plan, a way to pass intelligence. A romance was proposed by the military planners. The young lady would be introduced to an eligible bachelor and they would meet away from prying eyes. Plans of any military operation would be passed from the Adjutant's secretary to the Police. And of course, there would be a chaperone. Enter a young boy who would always be present with the couple. That was me. I never knew it, but I was an assistant spy!

My sister and I would go down from the Big House to the wonderful white sandy beaches of Port Dickson, and were often joined by a young man; all very calm and casual. We were free, no threat and having fun. I remember that wonderful beach, staying close to the shore, gathering shells in the shallow waters. And there was that young man, no uniform, who joined us occasionally.

The "Box Brownie", the first camera of the masses, was invented in 1900 and was essentially still in use in the 1950s. Black and white films were produced, with each negative measuring 2¼" square. It is those developed films that provide the evidence of a third party being with us on those occasions. I often wondered who had been able to take the few pictures of Jean and me at the beach. There are a couple we have of Jean and a handsome, eligible bachelor sitting on the beach, smiling happily; I guess I gathered that evidence. There were times when the venue would be changed and we were driven to the local shopping bazaar, where again information was exchanged; or the Land Rover would stop by the roadside and Jean would hand over documents from the Regiment to a courier. She recalls it still as very exciting for a 17-year-old woman, romance or not.

We are both very proud of the significant role played by our father, Captain Charles Gill MBE, in the battles for the freedom enjoyed by Malaysia today. The personal touch and compassion for the Malay people which he demonstrated in so many ways shaped us both. Jean lived in Malaysia and Singapore for the next 40 years of her life, her children were born there, and I have just made my second journey home to Mother Malaya in three years.

In returning to Port Dickson some 60 years after our espionage subterfuge to seek out our beach, I was advised to stay away as I could be disappointed. True, that beautiful beach was no more. Much of it had been destroyed by severe storms, and it had also been polluted by the industrialization. Far better to keep the memories in a jar and let nostalgia creep in from time to time. So as Jean and I share cherished memories, I know she is the spy that loves me still and that Port Dickson was the nerve centre of our operations on behalf of Her Majesty's Government.

CROSSING BORDERS

"Immigrant" is perhaps one of the most used nouns in the world today. I would not like to undertake a review of the adjectives that accompany that word, but I suspect many of them would not be on the kind side, thus pushing the word over the abyss into the dark divide. In today's world this is on everyone's mind. In discussion, even with the best of friends, you get a kaleidoscope of views each either illuminating or clouding the other. Open, closed, surrounded by sea, limited by mountains, Shengen rule in Europe, ancestral customs, right of birth... the list goes on. But how does that translate? Travel and immigration go hand in hand in as much there are rules to be observed, country controls at the many borders before we are each given the courtesy of stepping over the threshold. We are in another house and as such are no more than guests, welcomed by our host for a brief time.

On a lighter side, before the dawn of our mass communications, the great raconteur and actor Peter Ustinov was visiting Australia, that great vast country and former penal colony. At immigration on showing his passport he was reputedly asked "Do you have a criminal record, sir?" His response was "I thought that was a requirement." He was admitted.

I am an immigrant; Canada is now my home. How easy or difficult was it for this English person to leave for one of the great Commonwealth countries with such strong ties to the United Kingdom? Going back some 40-plus years, one would have thought it easy. Being recruited by a major Canadian Bank with guarantees in place for housing and health care meant the Government or tax-paying public were safe from me becoming a burden. Detailed medicals for my wife and me, references from past employers etc, two interviews with the Canadian Consulate and so on. Documents were in place for this six-month process and we were on our way to what was to become our new home. I had graduated from immigrant status to citizen, a simple process of following the rules. But as with all immigrants, I share the fact that I have left my homeland.

On my first visit to the UK after getting my Canadian passport, I handed it over at Immigration before joining the scanning life we all now inhabit. Like a kid in a candy store, I wanted the high of having a stamp in my passport. The UK agent read the first page which showed my birthplace as Northallerton, England, handed the passport back and said "Welcome home, sir". I took the passport, no stamp, then proffered it back and asked for a stamp of entry. He said "I am not allowed to touch your passport, sir; this is your country." What a let down!

On leaving I was miffed, so I decided to offer my British passport. The agent looked at the screen, who knew what notes were there, as there were no scans. His comment was "Hope you enjoyed your trip home sir. I see you came in on your Canadian passport." They knew! How did they do that?

During the period I was working in that lush, beautiful island nation of Trinidad and Tobago, I discovered one morning that five passports for the family had been stolen out of my car; not the best place to leave them. I called my contact at the Canadian High Commission (for once the phones were working) and was told to get pictures taken and signed off and they would chauffeur the required documents for completion to my office. By the time we got there the forms were waiting, so we filled them in, signed off and walked down to the CHC in Port of Spain. I had a chat with a few of the people, who were all pleased to help and gently chided me on the misfortune. That afternoon new passports were at my office and were afforded better custody in the future. Could you see that being done today, notwithstanding such a tech-savvy world?

While I was in Trinidad, a cousin asked to visit me from the UK. My response, "Sure, no problem, man. Just make sure you tell Immigration you are staying with me and that you here for vacation. Do not say anything. Nothing at all." The plane was early and even some 45 minutes later there was no sign of my cousin. I checked in with Immigration and they said they had been calling me. Yes, lines were out again. The head of Immigration, also a good friend, happened to be there that evening. Apparently my cousin, after a few rums trying to get into the spirit, was emboldened to tell Customs and Immigration that after a great flight and meeting many happy Trinidadians on the plane, sharing drinks and stories, that he would look for a teaching job while he was in Trinidad. After going into Immigration, where he had been detained, I told Ian that he was going to be put back on the flight. Once he got to the UK he could rebook and return. A day later he was back, uttered nothing but my name and had a wonderful shortened holiday.

In more recent history, when Carolyn and I were travelling through South East Asia I introduced her to the Pearl of the Orient, the island of Penang in Malaysia. We stayed in the north part of the island on a beautiful beach close by a village called Batu Fehringgi, an area I had known from childhood. We took time to do some laundry in the well-appointed hotel and to our surprise we also realised we had laundered two Canadian passports. I dried each page carefully with a blow dryer and placed tissue between the pages. They looked perfect.

When it came time to leave Penang, we crossed over to mainland Malaya by ferry and boarded a train from the small town of Butterworth bound for Bangkok. Our passports were in hand, all visas intact and we were on our way. We would sleep partially overnight after exiting Malaya some two hundred miles north at Padang Basar, the Malay/Thai border. The overall journey to Bangkok was some five hundred and sixty miles and we were looking forward to some sleep in our special seats, which made up into beds. All we had to do was get across the border.

On arrival at the station we had the amazing experience of two countries wanting to keep us. The Malays, who had to put an exit stamp on the passports, refused to carry out the task as they considered the passports damaged and said they should be replaced. They wanted us to go to the Embassy in Kuala Lumpur to get new passports, Logically one would think that as they had been happy to welcome us and their entrance stamp was clear, they would be just as happy to see us go. The icing on the cake was that the Thais were willing to welcome us and had their entry stamp ready, but legally they couldn't stamp the passports until Malaya showed an exit entry. There was a very noisy wrestling match between the two countries. We needed to get back on the train, which by now was running some 20 minutes late.

Finally I managed to get the senior Malay officer to one side. I just asked him to listen. Briefly I said my father had been a friend of Tunku Abdul Rahman, who was Malaysia's first head of Government and who had taken Malaya to independence from the British. The Tunku had occasionally come to our house, and I had known him as a young boy. This turned out to be the right move, as the awed officer shouted to his assistants to get the passports stamped and to help us board the train immediately. A little bit of shock and awe never hurt.

Wherever we go there are borders, rules and immigration/border patrols. There is no consistency, but there is a world to explore and time is of the essence. We must experience our shared planet and nature; there are borders to cross and new friends and experiences to enliven us on our journey as citizens of the world.

CHAPTER 15

WE LIKE IT SO!

A simple phrase, perhaps. A feeling of melancholy, a sense of holding on and not giving in to the anxiety of change? Or could it end up being the rallying battle cry in the raging fires of passion that accompany hard-fought political elections?

In the late 1970s and early '80s I was privileged to absorb the life and culture of that magnificent Caribbean country Trinidad and Tobago, courtesy of a work permit signed by the Prime Minister, Dr Eric Williams. It was there that a friendship developed between a man I will call CJ and myself that is as strong today as it was all those years ago. He provided a window to an incredible world.

I was in Trinidad the day the music died. On March 29th, 1981 Dr Eric Williams passed away. This giant of a man had cast both light and shadow on his homeland. From Queen's Royal College (QRC), in 1932, this son of Trinidad won a scholarship to Oxford University in the UK and was placed first in his class in honours history. His doctoral thesis was a brave and brilliant perspective entitled "The Economic Aspect of the West Indian Slave Trade and Slavery". Facinating! He was not afraid to tackle issues head on and his formidable memory, debating skills and powerful and erudite oratory steered him to the political posts of Chief Minister and Premier, until he became the first Prime Minister of an independent Trinidad and Tobago in 1962. In simple terms he was a force not only in his own country but within the Commonwealth of Nations. His national political party, the People's National Movement (PNM), was pivotal in Trinidad; there was no significant opposition.

But times change. Or do they? In the late 70s and early 80s there was a whispering breeze of potential for change. Another of Trinidad's talented men, Karl Hudson Phillips, was working closely, somewhat secretly, with his network of well-connected friends on the formation of a new political party, the Organisation for National Reconstruction (ONR). Karl was another graduate of QRC and his post-secondary education was at Cambridge. A brilliant lawyer, he went on to be Attorney General in Eric Williams' governments and in his later years was a judge in the International Criminal Court.

As an expatriate I could not actively participate or vote in government elections. That's as it should be. However, through my friendship with CJ, I became thoroughly familiar with the issues, passions and quest for change that were bubbling throughout the country. Dr Williams had wielded extraordinary power and was not to be questioned or challenged, and that became the modus operandi in politics and business. Karl Hudson Phillips decided to lead that charge for change and working industriously in the background was the articulate, well-connected and charismatic CJ.

I was fortunate to be a guest on a number of occasions at Karl's old family home in the heart of Port of Spain where this intellectual, charming, gracious and accomplished man shaped his vision. The close friends present were those that went on to make changes in future governments and to drive the economy forward while at the helm of major corporations. The talk was politics, but we also had history lessons through personal memories, shared experiences and great stories from brilliant minds and natural-born storytellers from the many walks of life who created a Trinidadian mosaic that is still present.

The year of 1981 in Trinidad was like no other. The mesmerising soulful brilliance of calypso, steel band competitions, dance, art and the bacchanalia that is the essence of the greatest Carnival on earth was centred around March 2nd and 3rd. It was time to rest, regroup and recover. And then March 29th loomed and the news spread throughout the island that Dr Eric Williams was dead. There was a sudden vacuum; the police and the military were out in force, stores and banks closed briefly. Shock reigned, and the island was stunned to silence. Dr Williams' funeral was worthy of the man. This founder of the Republic was laid in state in the Rotunda of the Red House and it seemed as though the whole populace worked its way through. I took my own family to pay respects, to be part of those touched by his life. This was a quiet, respectful affair with tears from men and women flowing silently.

But soon as the Government carried on, elections loomed, called for November 1981, and the ONR decided it would flex its wings. This was old-style politics. Candidates would go from village to village and town to town, speeches would be in halls, but more often in the open on a stage. Little tent cities developed and the crowds would gather well before the candidates started their popular rants, appeals of passion, throwing promises into the air, and they responded to arguments and agitation in like manner. These events were a festival in themselves.

I attended a number of tents with CJ, who was still working with me, and was not a part of the open politicking at this time. He had to be a little cautious about his job, but it was known he was a confidante of Karl Hudson Philips and so he did come in for some vocal challenges. One particular village we visited was Laventille. This is a hillside village to the east side of Port Of Spain and has been around since the 18th century, but it didn't thrive with the military camps and attempts at coffee growing failed. Laventille, through its history, became a place where people did not want to be. But it grew with labouring, domestic workers being the prime occupants. When we visited a few times you could see life was hard. Running water was scarce from lack of infrastructure, and drains were open. Women of all ages could be seen carrying buckets to the few areas with taps and hauling their heavily-laden buckets homeward. Electricity was virtually non-existent, and anything that was wired would suffer the interminable outages that were the norm in Trinidad. Telephones were usually hit and miss, and of course cellphones did not exist. Some of the wooden homes were built from wooden crates from Japan that had originally carried the imported cars. How easy for a politician to promise little and reap rewards!

But there was pride. You would never see a young girl or boy walking to school with an unpressed uniform or socks and shoes that were not white and always, always, hair was in place, whatever the style chosen. These children had the same education at the same schools as every other child; all were equal regardless of economics and their uniforms were a testament to that, as were their eventual successes in life. The schools are run the same way today, and every child has the chance to be the next Dr Williams.

So CJ and I arrived, with me of course being the only white person in that whole arena. But in Trinidad this did not matter.

I could banter with the best and the wonderful women were the most enjoyable to engage with. CJ and I recollect that often he would fare the worst. These were strong women. There appeared to be not too much love for the party he was identified with. The topic of water supply came up many times; how it could change, how old and tired the party of the venerated Eric Williams was and so on. Everyone was actively engaged and first names showed the friendliness. CJ was addressed as "Carlos". It was interesting to take the temperature of the place.

As we left one early evening the knock-out punch was landed. One well dressed, shall we say expansive lady, in bright clean clothes, was carrying two buckets of water from one of the few taps operating and wending her way up the hill. CJ gave her a friendly greeting as she passed and offered that this way of life could all change at the election. She stopped, put down her buckets, not a valuable drop spilled, kept her back to us and slowly bent forward and raised her dress – no underwear. Looking round, she caught us with her smile and said with some passion "we like it so!" In sharing stories this January, we both vividly recalled that visit to Laventille.

During the balance of the year I made a number of visits to the political camps around Port of Spain and in the smaller towns. Always welcomed and never treated with any suspicion, I enjoyed having conversations with all the men and women who made me welcome, shared their beer and food and would never take no for an answer. Great wit and humour abounded. I learned a lot about people and politics.

A few weeks before the 1981 General Election, CJ and I were having a chat in my office. I gave him an envelope, signed and with a seal. He was to keep this in the office vault until the election results were final. There was optimism in the new party he was "quietly" associated with. They believed they had a chance at minority government, or at worst forming the official opposition. There were 36 seats in the Parliament.

When CJ opened the envelope following the election, there was quiet shock. I had forecast 26 seats for the late Dr Williams' PNM Party, a majority of ten in a parliament of thirty-six seats. Carlos' fledgling party had zero. A talking point to this day for all politically-engaged cohorts. It always seemed the great calypsonians had the pulse of the country. Throughout that 1981/1982 period the truth of the matter was forecast by two legends of note. The Mighty Sparrow delivered "We like it so" and The Lord Kitchener was right on the mark with "Not a damn seat for Dem", a condemnation of the new ONR party.

CJ did eventually move into the public political sphere. He was appointed as a Senator and a Minister of Government in 2000. He went on to contest a seat in later in the year and again in 2001 as Parliament crumbled; winning both times, he was also Minister of Infrastructure Development and Local Government. CJ is now retired, but it is a pleasure and privilege to be with him wherever we go, a restaurant, in the street, and watch people approach him and thank him sincerely for what he personally did for them.

We have often recalled those memories and the pulse that was taken on the country by one from outside Trinidad who was welcomed by such wonderful people with a pride in their land and history.

CHAPTER 16

RICHARD AND MARIO

To this day, some forty years after we first met, CJ is one of my closest friends. He is, he has avowed, my brother. His children call me 'Uncle' and will not use my first name in talking with me despite my pleadings, and his wife of immeasurable talents and beauty recognises our unique relationship and uses the same language, saying "your brother misses you".

Our families had sons of a similar age, with my Richard and CJ's Mario. Last year, at Mario's fortieth birthday, a number of us were recalling some of the adventures of the young boys. Mario and his sister were enthralled with some of the stories and in particular one which we older adults recollected so clearly. We were gathered on a Saturday evening, with other close friends, at my home in Diego Martin, Trinidad after another adventurous day at Maracas Bay. It was a whole day of sharing, friendship, and families drawn together. It was also a time of political upheaval (when is it not?) in this beautiful country called Trinidad and all of us were very politically engaged at that time. There was tension between the haves and have nots and chasms drawn across racial lines, yet these people are all Trinidadian. It was the time when Trinidad had lost its first Prime Minister, Dr Eric Williams. Born in Port of Spain, he was educated locally and for six years at Oxford University. A great raconteur and historian, he was intimidating in debates. He ruled Trinidad from 1962 to 1981, taking it to Independence.

But back to the story. We educated adults decided to see what we could learn from the next generation, represented by Richard and Mario, who were about five years old at the time. What was their filter, what differences did they see, what was important in their lives, what benchmarks did they have? Their honesty and innocence surely could be the guide, as could their competitive natures. As we sat around the dining table our questions were fired out, not preplanned, and the boys were eager participants.

CJ: "Mario, what is one difference between you and Richard?"

Mario, looking around, looking at his friend, fingers to his lips, eyes lit up, recalling part of the beach day, responds "I can run faster than Richard".

We thought "is the gauntlet down? How competitive is this going to be?"

Alan: "Richard, what do think is a difference between you and Mario?"

Richard, having heard the answer of his friend, the faster runner, leapt smilingly into his response: "I can swim better than Mario. And I can swim under water". True.

The boys looked around for their accolades. They got them.

CJ: "Richard, give us another difference that you can see."

Richard, with our family dog by his side, looked at Mario and said "Bess, my dog, comes to the beach with us and even swims out to the rocks. Mario's stays at home." He looked around at the adults, saw our smiles and knew he had aced the test.

Alan: "Mario, you boys are pretty smart, what else do you see?"

Mario, looking across the table to where his mother, Glenda, held her one-year-old daughter, Candice, immediately jumped in with "I have a new baby sister, but I don't have a brother like Richard".

These boys were quite astute and again they received their applause with broad grins spreading across their innocent faces. Smiles were on ours too.

CJ: "Mario, there must be something else you can see every day you are together. What do you think, Richard?

Richard and Mario, looking at each other, shrugging shoulders, smiling, getting antsy as young boys do, wanting to get back to the important things in life, both answered "We go in different cars to the beach". Second answer: "We go to different schools".

As adults, we were learning the importance, or not, of their differences. The other adults joined in with their own thoughts and we all relearned the love these boys had for their utopian life, apparently risk free and to be enjoyed and shared. Oh, how we can love that innocence of youth! These moments allow us to recapture what we thought was lost.

Mario was blessed with beautiful dark skin like his father CJ, and Richard had the burden of my white English skin, not quite suited to tropical climates, even though it had been tested in Malaysia for eight years. But as my dermatologist tells me, "there is nothing wrong with English skin – in England!"

We lived for several years in CJ's country of Trinidad. It was a great gift and education for me to live within the intimacies of the beautiful Trinidadian culture and society and to be welcome in the homes of my friends and their families. I do return and connect all over again. We are more than friends. We are members of each other's families. We did not see colour in people, and nor did our children.

Childhood is tantalizing in the way it shapes you. My father absorbed so much of people, customs and civilizations from the time he spent in Africa, India, Burma (Myanmar) and Malaysia. In his own quiet way he was able to instil within me a deep respect for others. Those gifts were enhanced through my childhood years in Malaya, and have been cherished throughout life.

Within our various Malay households we employed Chinese, Indian (Tamil) and Malay people. Some had families living with them, babies and young children. There was no colour, but I was naive enough to believe there were no differences. But the latter could be and was embraced. My childhood days were a gift.

I did know in my first school in Malaysia that I was different from others. I got dropped off by car or military Land Rover while all my classmates, boys and girls, walked from the closest villages. And that was it. We learned together, played together, encouraged one another, took our first steps in writing, learning to form letters. My immediate desk friends were two Malay girls and a Chinese boy. Their first language was Malay and during our play times I enhanced my own ability to speak with them and in turn their own English language expanded. There was nothing we could not describe; we could always find the right word, no matter what the language. Our only difference in all that we shared was that their bilingual skills were better than mine. Local customs were explored and Christmases shared.

Fast forward thirty-plus years and my Brother CJ and I relieved that same joy of childhood innocence with our own children, who did not see colour and embraced differences. We have grown in culture and friendship. We are not innocents in our world, and we rejoice that we can share our common gift with others. "Brother" has no boundaries.

CHAPTER 17

GERALD AND CAROL

They walked away without so much as a backward glance

Many years ago, I was introduced to a young man who had a profound influence not only on my life but on all who crossed his path. He was born in the mid-1930s into a young family settling into their new home in a quiet, quintessential ancient market town in northern England; that part that is known as God's Own County by those born there. Life was relatively idyllic and complete when our young man, boy as he was then, received the gift of a sister. But within a short time dark clouds were rolling in, the clouds of war. Sabre-rattling, mesmerized crowds in Europe, people and lands pillaged; no one was left unscathed. Destruction was the norm in this apocalypse.

Life for many would never be the same again; this family was no different. The father joined the military and left for Africa, India and the hell that was Burma. Just prior to his leaving another son was born. The sister was in and out of hospital, wearing iron callipers on her legs for two years. The family home (three small bedrooms) was also earmarked by the government to temporarily accommodate three additional families escaping the London Blitz, and as part of the war effort the mother also had to make a contribution by working three nights a week at a local dairy. Not an easy life for anyone.

It was at this point, as an eleven-year-old, our young man contracted polio, a devastating disease but not uncommon in those times. Time in a sanatorium, isolation and paralyses, away from home, extreme pain, the loss of the freedom and joys of youth were his lot in life for a while, and the final result was a withered leg with no usable muscles. Childhood as he knew it was gone; but not his faith in his doctors, nor his fight to live a full life. The essence of who he was would win.

Crippled by his polio, our young man developed an authoritative walk, a swagger, if you will, thrusting the iron-braced leg ahead of him, balancing on it and swinging his body forward, then planting his good leg ready for the next pirouette. His shoes were always gleaming like polished glass. If the shortened and withered leg was to be a focus, then you would see the pride in the handcrafted shoes, a statement in itself: "I am not hiding". Broad of shoulder, dark-haired, sparkling grey eyes on which you would focus, you were at once drawn into the ambience of someone who would give you hope and faith. You were safe.

Our young man had graduated from medical school and specialized in orthopaedic surgery. It was time for him to give back in gratitude to those who had gone before and aided him. Always a man of faith, he was humble enough to know that his skills alone could not have changed, cured and saved the lives temporarily placed in his hands for care. It was impossible for his mind to accept that man alone was responsible. His own faith in his God became deeper. He carried this aura about him, gentle and not smothering, and you would gradually feel and would know you were in the company of goodness.

Life is never certain. Our young surgeon, leaving his hospital in the dawn following another night of operating and mercy, lost his life in a head-on collision immediately outside the front gates of his hospital. Death was instantaneous, as was the profound ripple of sadness that darkened the lives of those that knew him, but in time the goodness again took over.

Many years later a loving, dynamic, compassionate and quietly powerful woman came into my life. She was not my wife or my soulmate but a friend, a priest at a new church I was attending. While engaged in a business career that I thoroughly enjoyed, I was taking university courses in theology for fun, the pursuit of knowledge and certainly background in my own chosen faith. My friend and priest encouraged me, drew me into her circle and church family. We thrived as people and a church and expanded this growth into our community.

Carol, as she was known to all, had her own personal fights. Three battles against ovarian were won, and through all this she continued to minister. She always believed that we had more in us than we gave and that faith would see us through.

One Monday I was in her office and she opened a discussion about there being special dates when the church invited church members, not ordained but involved in theological studies, to deliver the sermon at services. The following Sunday, a short six days in the future, was one of those days. The context of the scriptural readings for the Sunday had in some way to be incorporated in the sermon so that a consistent message was delivered with the words being brought to life, and with the usual twinkle in her eyes and a matching smile she informed me that she would like me to deliver the sermon at all services the following Sunday.

My response was "Really?" I was somewhat amazed, but I knew I had been challenged. So I was tasked; refusing would not be a victory, it was not even an option with Carol.

Apparently I had lots of time. All I had to do was tell a story, weave it with scripture that made the story relevant and run it past her on the Thursday. Run it by her I did. I recall some of the comments of my dear friend: "Very good; a good essay, somewhat legalistic; good for debate; too theological, a certain lack of life, not enough passion" and so on. She got up from her chair, hugged me and said "It is there. It's inside. I trust you. I believe in you, you know the story already. I don't need to see what you will share. I'll pray for you and see you on Sunday." She did.

I struggled, worked diligently, created, destroyed, resurrected the old and tried the obtuse. Results were troubling, measured against the expectations of trust and belief and the charge that apparently I knew the story already. On the Friday I had something workable, but not good. There was nothing more I could do except trust and pray; yes certainly pray, as I needed all the help I could get.

That evening I went into a deep, peaceful sleep. I awoke, quietly not startled, to see that sitting on the side of my bed was the young doctor, the man of faith. He slowly turned his head and broad shoulders, drew me in with those mesmerizing grey eyes, his smile in place and said compassionately and convincingly "Use me". I did not speak. We stayed like that for a moment, close together. I closed my eyes and then he was gone.

On waking, I was refreshed, energy bursting. I took my pen and pads of paper and wrote of the young man's struggles, the joy in his calling, his faith and his victory over adversity. All were interwoven with the scriptures for the Sunday. The writing came easily, and so did the message on that Sunday. The story was there, told with meaning and passion. It worked. I could not have done it alone.

About a year later, we lost Carol. What a difference she had made in so many lives. She had that special spirit and faith that wraps you in a cloak of comfort, just as with our doctor. They had changed lives with their gifts and strengths, which they acknowledged as not theirs alone.

One night a few months later, I awoke after only a few hours' sleep but fully rested and peaceful. There at my bedside, comfortably sitting together, arm in arm were the young doctor and priest. They were smiling with joy, sharing a secret, eyes glistening. Then, with small positive nods of satisfaction, they affirmed me and the story they had both given me. Turning slowly, a warm, meaningful look between them, they stood together, restored, no infirmities, no sickness. Then, arms linked, they walked away without so much as a backward glance.

It was a joy to see my brother and my minister again.

Gerald and Carol changed lives for the good. With their gifts they made our world a better place and yet in this life they never met.

Dr Gerald James Gill MB. BS, February 28 1933 – September 26, 1970 England

Rev. Carol Ann Skidmore, November 17 1943 – August 10 2008, Canada

CHAPTER 18

THE PASSAGE OF TIME

Finding the calm, the presence within, that space which allows you to move forward and having these desires all gel together has been a difficult task of late. Not dark, but neither is there that beam of light that draws you as a moth to the flame of expression. My writing has stagnated somewhat and despite the ever-sharp presence of my Tombow 2B pencils, ready to create, racing over fresh territory, I have not been able to do my share. The paper is blank.

Perhaps the message is simple and the tools of my craft have been waiting for this time when I can close with those words of our forefathers: "well done my good and faithful servant". They know.

I think I have within me a few more vignettes. Certainly life moves forward and will bring with it new experiences to share. But for now the finished works deserve a better place than resting, untouched, unseen, in their comfortable box or on a computer drive. One hopes that what is shared in the public domain will allow an appreciation of days gone by and act as a prompt to others that they have stories to tell of the worlds into which they have ventured, the people that have made a difference and an appreciation of the diversity of us all. We were but children once and absorbed all around us. We bloomed through the tragedies of wars and hopefully emerged better for that. We have been able to experience the generosity and grace extended to us by those in whose countries we were guests for a short but hopefully life-changing time. We are still grateful for those opportunities. We can breathe in life. There is nothing finite here.

We are not living in a dream, a vacuum, and as time moves irrevocably forward the harsh realities of life have to be faced, even though we may tuck them away when it suits us.

My brother in law, Darien, has been in a private home with twenty-four hour care for the last few years. He is lovingly and well cared for and has family visits three or four times a week from his wife, who has shared a wonderful life with him for over sixty-five years. He cannot carry on a conversation or feed himself and we do not know what that once magnificent brain is thinking. Expression is by the blink of an eye, slowly, a small smile or perhaps the gentle touch of a hand, his own squeeze of reassurance that he wants to share. It is as if a feather glides over your skin.

Yet when I saw him recently after two years, and as I approached his bed he clearly said "Oh, Alan". There was a small smile and his hand slowly brushed mine. Alone together, I talked of my life, our past, my still great passion and love of cricket. I told him some tales of the latter and he managed to turn his head a fraction, smile and again brush my hand with his strong feather-like grip. I use "strong" as I can only imagine the immense effort it took, but he willed it for us. I left him, promising to return in another two years from beyond the Atlantic.

My sister Jean bears this separation alone, but with the atypical powerful strength and stoicism of the Gill women who came before, Granny Gill and our own mother. We continue to share our stories and anecdotes as known tales continue to pop up. There is joy in this; we know who and what moulded us. But in that sharing I have sensed these particular tales of my time, The Lost Colonial Boy, are perhaps for us alone and not to be extended to others in my writing.

Darien at 87, Jean at 84 and me the much, much younger brother at 75 have shared our love of our worlds and people. It has been a privilege for us to have lived and made our homes throughout our lives with family in different countries. England, Kenya, Scotland, New Zealand, Trinidad, Canada, Singapore and Malaya have provided a richness and variety. I suppose we should also add my father's military service in some African countries together with India and Burma (Myanmar) in the mix, as they too influenced our lives. But it is England, the place of our births, and Asia, with Singapore and Malaya, and its diverse peoples, religions, histories and mysteries that shaped us. Mother Malaya still calls, and we cannot forget our Roman and Viking blood from our small island of England.

Jean has a photo on her dresser of her and me at Bill Bang's rubber estate, Kelantan, Malaya taken in 1948. I am about six inches below her shoulder. In my 2019 visit to her home in Scotland, we took a similar pose. In this one she just reaches my shoulder, but as she reminds me, "You are still my younger little brother". Seeing these photos side by side, decades joined together, suggested to me "all is well" and our shared memories as captured are safe and real. There may well be more to come, but that can rest comfortably just between the two of us.

I will continue to treasure my 2B Tombow pencils, remember their effortless glide along light lines on unmarked paper, the resulting comfort and encouragement they provided in bringing thoughts to life. For now, we can rest.

I wrote this piece in July 2019. Darien passed peacefully at seven in the evening of Saturday September 14th, 2019. What better parting could two friends have wished for? I can still see his smile and surely feel his feather-like touch.

To complete the passage of his life I have undertaken to take his ashes to Singapore and Malaya, the birth places of our lives together.

Maud and Alan (at The Big House)

Maud. The Big House, Port Dickson

The Gardens (at The Big House)

Maud (at The Big House)

Alan (at The Big House)

Charles (at The Big House)

Jean and Alan, Port Dickson Beach

Alan in Penang

Sir Henry Gurney's Car

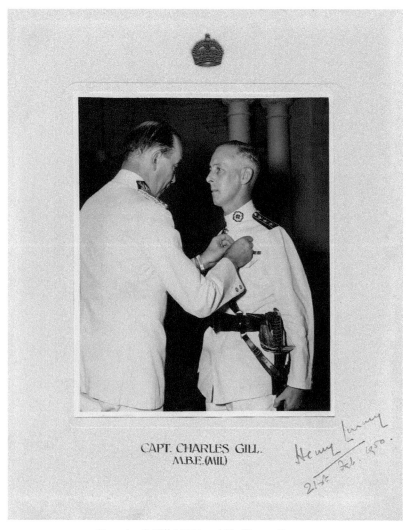

Captain C.Gill MBE and Sir Henry Gurney

George the Sixth _by the Grace of God of Great Britain, Ireland and the British Dominions beyond the Seas, King, Defender of the Faith and Sovereign of the Most Excellent Order of the British Empire to Our trusty and well-beloved Charles Gill Esquire Captain (temporary) (Quartermaster) in Our Army The Green Howards_ **Greeting** _Whereas We have thought fit to nominate and appoint you to be an Additional Member of the Military Division of Our said Most Excellent Order of the British Empire We do by these presents grant unto you the Dignity of an Additional Member of Our said Order and hereby authorise you to have hold and enjoy the said Dignity and Rank of an Additional Member of Our aforesaid Order together with all and singular the privileges thereunto belonging or appertaining_

Given at Our Court at Saint James's under Our Sign Manual and the Seal of Our said Order, this Eighth day of April 1949 in the Thirteenth year of Our Reign

By the Sovereign's Command

Grand Master

Grant of the dignity of an Additional Member of the Military Division of the Order of the British Empire to Captain (temporary) (Quartermaster) Charles Gill. The Green Howards

Royal Citation Charles Gill

Red Barns, Redcar

Alan, 1st row, 3rd from right

Gerald, 3rd row, 3rd from right

Alan, 2nd row, 3rd from right

Churchill, Bell and T.E. Lawrence

Gertrude Bell Plaque, Red Barns

School crest

Sir William Turner's School

Alan, 1st row, 3rd from right

Alan, 2nd row, 3rd from left

Charles' Garden in Darlington

Maud and Charles

Whisky, the faithful companion

Charles and Driver Kota Bharu

Maud and Alan 1st Home

Charles and Alan

Alan, new home

Maud and Jean

Alan

Alan and Friend

Charles, Bill Bangs, Alan and Jean

Maud and Charles

Jean and Alan

Bill Bangs Garden

CHAPTER 19

A VOICE FROM THE PAST

Charles Allen is a highly-regarded British author, historian, biographer and uniquely, an oral historian. His writings bring to life the Imperial history of the Raj in India and the British influence in South East Asia in the nineteenth and twentieth centuries. I am sure that his birth in India, where his parents had lived for many years, were a great catalyst in his understanding of the natural influences of those societies.

One of his books, *Tales From the South China Seas*, is particularly poignant for me. In part it focuses on Malaya, now part of Malaysia, my lifetime home of choice. Charles also worked for the British Broadcasting Corporation and received accolades for his oral histories and interviews, which then formed the basis for some of his books.

In the fall (autumn) of 2019 I was reading this fascinating book on culture, people, history and geography, essentially life, when suddenly the name of Bill Bangs appeared. As I went through the stories there was Bill again and again. This was a gift which brought my old family friend back to life. Wonderful tales and memories rekindled.

In the acknowledgements section of the book there was a reference to the Imperial War Museum in London, which held many of Charles Allen's oral history recordings which profiled not only the wars and life in Malaya but interviews with Bill. This was a huge gift. I wrote to the IWM requesting information and access. Surprisingly, there was a reply within days. Their ruling was yes I could have access but would first have to obtain permission from that behemoth the British Broadcasting Corporation, as it held the rights. So off I went again to the BBC, and they amazingly replied within the week giving approval, which I then had to copy to the IWM. After reading and signing a six-page legal document, which by my interpretation meant I would be sent to the Tower of London if I messed up, I received three digital file recordings of Bill Bangs having conversations with Charles Allen. Brutal frankness about Changi Jail and the Death Railway, culture, people, religion, rubber plantations, it was all there. This was about my early home, my life and the country and people I loved. Bill had come to life.

As I listened for the first time I was alone in the quiet of my home. I sat by my small hundred-year-old oak desk, switched on the computer and closed my eyes. I could sense Bill in the room, that same soft cultured voice, a gentle giant of a man telling a captivating tale. At the end of that session I looked at one of the shelves of photographs and there we were: Bill, my father, my older sister Jean and me sitting on the steps of our Malay home in Kota Bharu, Kelanten, Malaya, downriver from Bills rubber plantation.

Visions and memories are treasured.

CHAPTER 20

Dying embers

On the fringe of Northern Ontario, up at the cottage, nestled on the lake, in the true darkness of night, not illuminated by city lights, we occasionally have wonderful wood fires from stocks of our trees, those that died and yet still can give us the warmth of life. Beautiful smells. Marshmallows are good! As the fire dies the embers, those smouldering, crackling pieces of wood that remain, glow even more brightly until they too are claimed by the dark. It is over. But above, if we gaze carefully into infinite darkness, are the brightest of stars, flashing their messages of hope. The more we stare, the more there are. We are transfixed; this is what infinity is like.

It is written "the days of our lives are three score years and ten". Dating is around 480 BC for this writing, a Psalm, so that was essentially some 2500 years ago. Not a bad forecast still! Every day we are in the now, which is suddenly the past, and that future which was ahead of us is suddenly the present. The three score years and ten sees its future diminished every second, but fear not, surely once the barrier is broken we start again. We all know that the past and future are illusions and all we have is now. We own the past, we created it, we are responsible; the future is beyond us, and that leaves us in the present. We cannot avoid the now.

That is the easy road. Now come the most difficult challenges, the parts that most of us dwell on, retrospection and introspection. Have we made a difference to benefit our fellow travellers? What did we learn from those who guided our earliest years, what was learned from ancient history? Do we see the future as bathed in light, do we want a place in what is before us, or do we yearn for what once was? Is this time, this time right now, as good as it gets, or do we judge it as a failing?

I know to Whom I am answerable through infinity. I have my ancestry and ancestors to honour for all they taught me, and within me I have my own life experiences that made me and continue to mould me still. I know I made a difference in some worlds. But the greatest gift I received is that I have lived this life in the period that was chosen for me. That I would not change.

So to get back to the three score years and ten. Mine are past, so my future is guaranteed! Would I like to have lived in a different era, absolutely not. I have been blessed; this world shared its vast diversity and people from all backgrounds with me. What have I been able to bring to the table? Would I like to be starting off on another three score and ten, given what I see before us in this world? A very firm "Absolutely not!" I abhor what I see before us of the way we treat people, the ongoing unlearned lessons of our inhumanity to our brothers and sisters throughout our shared planet. That will be the essence of our destruction; we reap what we sow, we have not learned. So this short exposé is me on me, little snapshot vignettes that frame the experiences that remain with me today. Each of these memories will form other stories which are longer in their telling, more personal, and hopefully open our eyes to the infinite variety of who we are.

Birth

The country of my birth gave me history, the conquering Romans, the Vikings, the Normans, Germans and the marauding Scots, Dutch and Spanish and so on. We had the Tudor and Elizabethan eras with their arts, exploration and world voyages, worldwide trade and religious battles. Then came the gradual devolution into a parliamentary system that spread throughout the world, with continents won and continents lost. And of course the thinkers, literary giants, artists, sculptors, inventors and the great political leaders of all stripes. The past still lives on; this small island kingdom was shaped by its past and has not as yet sought to eradicate it. "Great" is firmly part of Britain. Hard to believe my father's great grandparents were born in Napoleonic times, my own grandparents lived through Victoria's reign and here I am today, in the now. Quite a stretch.

My father

The kindest, most gentle man I have ever known. What an incredible man! He introduced me to history, books and choices, and cherished me, showing me our human sameness as I grew up as a child among Malay, Tamil and Chinese people. He guided gently without me knowing. Principles were instilled that have been with me since that time. The graciousness he taught me was so visible when I visited Malaysia four years ago. I shared my childhood background with some Malay people I had never met before. One, a young man, turned to me, placed his palms gracefully together, bowed slowly before me and said, "my people thank you for your father's service to our country." What an accolade! I am so very grateful for the way my life was guided.

My teachers

Those brave men who came back from the horrors of the Second World War and shared their true passions were my teachers, and some had aged more than their true years. Their love of history from British, European and a world perspective, geography as an opening to the world and its people, the precision of the sciences and maths and the literature from all ages back to Homer; they brought it all to life, passionately. Their love of sports in which they passed on their skills was a gift to us. They determined we would rise to be the best and not have the joys of friendly combat turned into a contest that stole the best years of our lives. We were challenged, we believed, we were the best. In our minds we still are.

My love of books and words

Perhaps this developed by osmosis. During the Second World War regular shipments of books left England from my family to wherever my father was in the world: Africa, India, Burma and eventually Malaya. The packages retraced his steps and eventually caught up with him. He loved his books. At home, in those away years, I was always read to every night by my brother and sister, and in my very early years in South East Asia there was a circle of four of us reading, again every night. The scene is firmly set in my mind. Years and years of reading, absorbing, questioning and developing the love of the written word still mesmerizes me to this day. This created an enquiring mind which cannot be stilled. Books and words and the people that love them are always a joy to me.

Newspapers, debate and provocative thoughts

At my boarding school we had three newspapers delivered every day. *The Times*, the establishment newspaper read all over the world, and two independent middle of the road papers, one leaning slightly left and one politically right. At lunch and beyond we were often engaged in debate, by our teachers, on any newsworthy item, and we had to be prepared. Our minds were forever challenged and our personal views had to be developed, with no sitting on the fence. Respect for opposing views, no shouting, no overriding comments, just very simply "listen with respect and respond in kind". Another gift to us, and our eyes were opened. We were not narrow in focus, we were worldly. It was surely a testament to the founding father of our school in the 1600s, Sir William Turner, as previously mentioned, who believed in the education of young minds even for the poor, who had no means for schooling except for that provided through his benevolence.

Thoughts, words and deeds

These, in part, can be the essence of who we are as a people. The edict of "Primum non nocere" (first do no harm), as enshrined in the Hippocratic Oath, words which, while not directly spoken by my father, were an integral part of who he was as a man and leader; hard to believe for a military man who had witnessed the worst of the worst in the theatres of war. He guided me and I hope, that when I put together the thoughts, words and deeds needed in communicating with others, those lessons come to the fore. I trust I can show the respect they deserve. It is a simple edict which, if practised over and over again, will make us all better people and hopefully create a more enlightened world.

I simply abhor what I see today that festers in all parts of our world, countries and neighbourhoods. We have forgotten the basics of life. We have people shouting, not thinking and the loudest of all are those who know more and more about less and less. They stir the flames of intolerance and hatred behind their disguise of punditry and their opponents are just a mirror image. We dig our trenches and take aim at each other with no thought as to the destruction we create, and allow wounds to fester. Within my lifetime this is perhaps among the worst of times and the cauldron building up may set off terrible strife that could have been averted if due respect had been given to thoughts, words and deeds.

A life too short

Three score years and ten. Not in the case of one young man, not even close; thirty-seven was my brother's final score. I shared twenty-six of those treasured years.

Jawaharlal Nehru postulated: "the hand that is dealt you represents determinism; the way you play it is free will". I was privileged to see that in play. I learned of crippling polio that robbed a young man of youth, the forever sunny days of endless youthful summers, and left him lame with an iron on his leg for the rest of his life. Surgery followed, attempts to repair that torqued body and make it more compliant to the physics of movement. The norm was time spent away at school and university in three-storey heritage buildings where access was the same for everyone; you walked up and down, no pampering elevators in sight.

Sports were not lost; he played badminton, table tennis and a little cricket, every move a masterful and unique feat of choreography. Playing bridge, the stakes were high and winnings usually raked in. And behind all this he was a Dean's scholar who graduated with his close friends with medical degrees and specialized in orthopaedics. Yes, in his mind it was time to give back, to use the gifts he had on loan in this life. He was a gentle man whose quiet grace and grey eyes, full of life, commanded gentle attention in every room he entered; a peaceful experience. I was the centre of that attention in every way; I soaked it in, and still do to this day.

I am so very grateful that I had at least I had those few years with my brother. Tough shoes to fill? Not at all. He still wears them!

People and places

It seems easier to say "people and places" than the other way round, but in truth it is always the places that come first. Born in a small prosperous town in Yorkshire, England, I had uncles, aunts, a brother, a sister and my grandmother. By four years of age I had sailed the oceans to South East Asia and made my home among Malay, Tamil, Chinese and a small number of British children, all friends, girls and boys. I did not realise it but I was a minority, in the common languages used (until I mastered Malay) and skin tone for sure. Such blessed innocence! That was my home on both coasts of Malaya for the next eight years. I returned to England and lived my life at boarding school for another eight years, returning only to my parents during vacation time. I loved every minute; fantastic sports programmes and education of the highest quality. We learned to be independent and respectful of those we lived with; we respected their space, their time, their gifts and struggles. We had ambitions. We were the next generation. It was the late fifties, and we gave birth to the so called 'Swinging Sixties' and were the light after the darkness of the Second World War.

For me England was not changing fast enough, so after a few years with sport and certainly work as a young banker I was recruited in the UK by a Canadian company and I bit the bullet and made Alberta my home. From there Toronto beckoned and also time in the Caribbean. Friends from diverse backgrounds materialized. Travelling had served me well.

My closest friend, no holds barred, spirited debates, philosophical and political arguments carried out with dignity, and a man and his family I have treasured for some forty years is a Trinidadian I will call CJ. We see each other in the USA or Trinidad and it is heartwarming when I talk with his wife and she says "Your brother misses you, give him a call." I do.

And then there is our winter home in St Petersburg, Florida. I almost had to put in the three score years and ten before I could qualify for residence. This is a home to an eclectic group from all walks of life. Key to my selfish pleasure is a small group of men and women pursuing their passion for connecting with each other through art, sculpture, memoirs, novels, plays, poetry, learning, stimulating conversation and above all safe, caring and firm friendships.

We are all in the "now". The future and the past all have untold treasures, and as we mine and share we are all enriched.

The destruction we see before us may not be ours to own; we can leave the culpability elsewhere. It may seem the embers are dying, but we can still light the flames. Perhaps we can take Enobarbus' tribute to Cleopatra and modify it slightly in saying, "Age shall not wither, nor custom stale their infinite variety". Or more violently, as Dylan Thomas raged, "Do not go gentle into that good night". I won't! The embers create a new fire. There are stars above and there is always, always infinity.

CHAPTER 21

Cricket, lovely cricket - the love affair of a lifetime

There was a shout from the bowler, "One handed off the wall, Gilly!" and the batsman was out to a great catch as the tennis ball ricocheted off the wall of the fives court and was grasped and held. "He's out! Good ball, Tom!" Always shouts of joy, excitement and encouragement. Just another form of adapting the great game of cricket to suite the environment.

The players this time were six boys aged eleven to seventeen testing their skills in a fenced-off area which held a racquet court and another wider area probably the size of three badminton courts. The fencing also protected the sacrosanct gardens of flowers and vegetables that surrounded the play area, the gardens being patrolled and nurtured by the Headmaster, a man who would also occasionally join us. In our space, he became a target. We occasionally lost balls on the old private railway track, which had belonged to the industrialist Sir Hugh Bell and whose home was now our residence.

We were boarders at Red Barns, which housed thirty-plus of us students who attended Sir William Turner's Grammar School (known as Coatham) in Redcar, North East Yorkshire, England. The school itself probably had five hundred pupils. The minimal spare time we had, when not studying, was spent on games. We were innovative and our cricket players at any time were mixed in age; the daily grouping would differ from one day to the next. The true form of the game was enjoyed by those of who went on to represent the school, representative teams, league cricket and above. We had dedicated teachers and coaches, all of whom had their own passions and were willing to pass them on to us.

This was not my first introduction to the game. My soul has been enriched by the love of this sport which first revealed itself to me in the mid-nineteenth century some ten thousand miles from the place of my birth. The game has been a tough taskmaster, moody and difficult at times, joyful, energising on the other spectrum. It has brought love and heartbreak, lifted one up to the heavens and always, always tugged at the heart.

Cricket is an old, old game started some five hundred-plus years ago in England. The basics are still there, a bat, a ball, and a grass pitch, the latter having no specific dimensions. Like all games it translates to being played in back yards, streets, the beach and anywhere you can find the tools and the passion. Surprising to many is that cricket, with 2.5 billion adherents, is the second most popular sport played in the world following soccer, with its 4 billion.

I was not introduced to cricket in England but rather on the grassy lawns of the old colonial Runnymede Hotel, alas no more, in Penang, Malaysia in the late nineteen forties and fifties. The Runnymede was home to a number of military officers' families whose children aged eleven and up were educated during term time at a British boarding school in the Cameron Highlands on the mainland. A military convoy would escort the students into the hills several times a year and would be part of the security on return at the end of term. The Malay Communist offensive was still active.

Among these students were Tim and Alec, who learned about cricket at school. They returned with this gem and shared it with us younger folk. My father had already had the basics of the real tools for us shipped from the UK; bats, wickets and balls. No longer did we need to have our roughly-sawn bats and wooden stakes for wickets; we entered the real world. In short order we had to use tennis balls, not true cork balls, poached from the hotel, due to the many people walking around our magnificent ground and of course the windows and doors on the lower level of the hotel were always a target for our misguided shots. On many an evening a few Officers would join us and tried to teach us and show off their inordinate skills learned on some of the hallowed grounds of England's old public schools.

We were ahead of our time in that we recruited, if that is the right word and indeed it was perhaps the other way round, a number of girls who had equal if not better skills from their ongoing games of rounders and tennis. And so in the evenings for a couple of years the Runnymede yielded part of its beautifully-trimmed greenery to the inspired youngsters. We learned the basics and they stayed as basics until we all eventually returned to England and if fortunate attended a school where cricket was a major sport. There the true challenges of gaining skills with coaching began. In addition we then had our own County teams to follow and players to hero worship and very wishfully emulate.

Sport at school was seasonal. The typical school year was divided into three terms; from the beginning of September to late

December, then from early January to April and the last term, the summer term, would be from about the third week in April to the last week of July. Essentially the outside school sport in the winter and spring terms was rugby, but in the warm, ever-changing summer months, cricket was king.

We played pick-up games during recess, chalking the stumps on a wall, designating which part of the playground counted for a certain number of runs, and while having fun we all played to win. There would be official coaching taking place and practice games for those of us fortunate enough to make the school sides. We worked our way up as we aged and moulded into the teams, known as Bantam, Junior Colts, Senior Colts, Second Eleven, First Eleven.

Ultimately in the final years of the school, starting in 1963, the 'Big Side', which was essentially an amalgamation of the latter two teams, was developed. This made sense as academics would often cut into the availability of top players. Weekly there would be an afternoon game against another school team and the same would happen on a Saturday. At the more senior levels we would travel to other schools with long-standing history in North Yorkshire and the County of Durham. All vast learning experiences that forever cemented the game into my soul.

As boarders at Sir William Turner's School, the end of term would see us return to our disparate homes across the UK, where we were separated from the community and camaraderie we had built up over the school terms with other boarders, day pupils and especially team mates. Cricket for me could not be found in those very early years at home, except when my father took me by bus to see some of the county games. They were few, but I treasured every one and got to see and recognise some of the players I had read about in the papers; the greats that played for their county and possibly England. I fondly remember those very special, kind days with my father; there was an understanding and quietness which bonded us. Alas the great Sir Len Hutton had retired before I saw him, but noteworthy and known to all true followers of the game to this day were Fred Truman, Brian Close and Ray Illingworth.

The world changed when I turned sixteen. My father was able to secure a summer job for me, as a full-time student, with the town of Darlington. At the same time he contacted someone in his office who played league cricket locally and arranged for us to meet at a cricket ground, Haughton, very close to our home. I now had money in my pocket, a bicycle, and an opportunity perhaps to join an adult team, although I was quite young, A couple of net practices later, I was invited to join and play for the Haughton Cricket Club. I had a few good years there until I left the area following school to take an assignment in banking in Leeds.

Key in my life at this time in Haughton were Herbie Innes and Michael Scott. Herbie and Mike were eight years older than me but took me under their respective wings. Herbie and his wife Barbara became a second family. Mike, the fun-loving bachelor who lived in the nearby village, showed me the fun side of life, nights of dominoes and the introduction to good northern draught beer. He was a good friend and we lost him too early. I always travelled with Herbie and Barbara to away games and on a regular basis had a Sunday tea with them when not playing. I was with them both when their daughter Jayne was born. This is a relationship I have treasured. Barbara died some years ago, but Herbie still lives in the same home I first visited him in some sixty years ago and where I still visit him from Canada whenever I am in England. He never fails to bring out his cricket memorabilia, scoring book, newspaper clippings and then recalls the good times with wonderful anecdotes that stir the memory. The world is a small place.

I never met Herbie's father, who was killed on the Burma Death Railway by the Japanese in the Second World War. However, in visiting Kanchanburi War Cemetery in Thailand in 2013, I was able to pay my respects to Herbie Innes; Bombardier H. Innes, Royal Artillery, killed on 13 September 1943. A journey Herbie was never able to make, but I was grateful I had done that in his place. I like to think it closed a circle for him.

And so to Leeds, a major city in Yorkshire that also had everything to offer a cricket junkie. It is the headquarters of the Yorkshire County Cricket Club, a team that produces legends to this day, whose home ground was Headingley. In winter months there were indoor "nets", practice areas for batsmen and bowlers, and my bank team and another club I was associated with used the facilities. It couldn't get any better. The great Yorkshire coach Johnny Lawrence was often on site and the inimitable Sir Geoffrey Boycott, when not touring, would practice and lap up the hours with anyone who cared to bowl at him. In season I played on a Sunday for the bank team, picked from the myriad of offices in the area, On Saturday there was league cricket and mid-week some knockout competitions. Special invitational games plus a trip once a year to London for a long weekend as a player on the bank's northern team were also in play. It was a great life doing what I loved. It was also the period when I met the other love of my life, but that's another story.

After three years I returned to Darlington and the Haughton Cricket Club and one other club. Friendships rekindled and new ones made. Another three years later I was in Nottingham and playing League cricket, again immersed in nets, representative games, a bank team and a good league. Great camaraderie and friendships were enjoyed, especially with the late Gordon

Stringfellow, a friend and team mate, an outstanding bowler who in later life was the scorer for Nottinghamshire County Cricket Club. It was fitting that at his funeral as the procession drove by the Trent Bridge Cricket Ground, the tall industrial cranes dipped their long metal necks in tribute to this man. It was here that my regular playing days ended. I was recruited by a Canadian Bank and emigrated to Canada. There was very little cricket in the Western Province of Alberta in those days. The desire and the love never died, but the actual playing did.

My first choices on leaving the UK were South Africa, Australia and New Zealand, as those countries had wonderful cricket culture and histories. It was a tough decision to head east, but Canada won out primarily because it was easier to return to England in case of any family emergency. How prescient this was; I was back in England by the end of October, having landed in Edmonton on July 9th. My older brother Gerald had been killed in a car accident.

But the game is within me still. Its glory never fades, new formats excite, new world-class players are heralded, and yet the reputations and sheer genius of the old world players never shrinks. Players today are in awe of the history of cricket; the knights of old live on and challenge these players to join them in their deeds.

In these my later years, still "Not Out", technology allows me to relive the glory years of Truman, Illingworth, Close, Boycott, Sobers, Lara, Hall and Griffith, Marshall and Valentine, Warne and Benaud, Lock and Laker, Kohli and Dhoni and the excitement of new players in a different cricketing world. That is nostalgia, but today's tests and short form games are beamed at me from anywhere in the world. There is still an adrenaline rush with the sheer power of today's cohort. But, as a Yorkshireman and without prejudice, the greatest delight was to see the sheer power, might and skill of Fred Truman putting all his strength, power and guile on display and cementing his reputation as "T'finest fast bowler that ever drew breath".

Thank you all, gentlemen and ladies, for my dreams to be realised time and time again. I may not be physically in Headingley, Trent Bridge, Scarborough, Kensington Oval Barbados or the Queen's Park Oval Trinidad, but I am there in spirit.

CHAPTER 22

A SEPTUAGENARIAN'S LETTER HOME

Dear Dad,

Yes, it has always been "Dad". When I write of you, talk of you, to others it always seems to be "my father". I don't really know why but I guess that "Dad" as a name, like Charles or Alan, is more affectionate, although in telling a story to others we default to "my father". Well, you are Dad and always were in my phone calls and compulsory weekly, letters home from boarding school. It was "Dear Mom and Dad" and I am sure the order was reversed from time to time.

And so here we are some forty-five years on from the time we lost you, far too young. But I guess life took its toll, losing your own father at an early age, not in, but after, World War One. You as the eldest stood up and did odd jobs with my uncles and helped your diminutive but powerful mother, Granny Gill. Funny, how in later years you and even a couple of the brothers referred to her as Granny. Then there was the start of a good family life in your beloved Northallerton, where your three children were born. When World War Two arrived you served in far-off lands, followed by another war in Malaya.

You were often gone, but I didn't know any different. Your elder son, my brother Gerald (I think we'll use Jim from now on) whom I still can't remember in those very early days was crippled by polio and, yes, we lost him too soon abut twenty years later. I think that was the final straw for you, but you soldiered bravely on. Just Jean and me left now, but of course you know that.

My earliest recollection of you is when Jean, Mom and I got off the ship in Singapore in the late '40s and there you were. That greeting is still entrenched in my mind and I can fondly recall that day from some photos we had.

Our life in Malaya was enthralling. It was a war that went by another name, an Emergency. Sometimes you were there and then you were gone, but I can recall so much of the time spent with you. Your driver Aziz would drive your Land Rover; he took us everywhere, to your military camp, the local markets, the coast to pick up fresh fish, and he used to speak Malay with me. In the end I was the most fluent in the family.

You took me on walks through the small towns and markets. You always wore a white open neck-shirt when not in uniform and always, always, there was a pipe in your hand. You opened up every culture to me and I learned a respect for people, their beliefs, their ways of life. I treasure to this day those times with the Malay, Chinese, East Indian and yes, old English cultures. Those lessons served me well all through life. I return to those old roots every few years and breathe in their welcoming warmth. To this day I relish that gift you gave me. I think you would be proud.

Jean, being nine years older than me, has regaled me with great stories, family life and so on of what went on in all those years of living on the east and west coasts of Malaya and Penang. What an amazing man you were; no wonder one of the lines on your citation for a military award has the words "his devotion to duty has earned for him the respect and affection of all races in the force". I am so proud you are my dad.

It must have been hard to be away from family and your home town of Northallerton in God's Country, as we still call Yorkshire. Jim had polio, and when we left England and he had to stay behind for schooling. You must have missed him when you were away in the war years. Jean of course was with us in Malaya; she even had the role of spy and worked in your military office from time to time. You have to know how much I love her stories of our lives with you in Malaya.

You were a military man, highly respected by your fellow officers and perhaps more importantly by those you led, a man of great and quiet strength honoured by your country. When you left the military you were only fifty-one. I learned much later that your senior commanding officers had tried to dissuade you from that choice, but you were adamant. King and country had taken part of your life, and now it was time for family. Had you stayed, no doubt you would have been away even more. It was only later that I realised what a huge sacrifice that was for you. You never showed it.

When Malaya was finished you were still in the military and involved in repatriating soldiers and equipment from various parts of the Middle and Far East. But you still put us first. Education was important to you, and it was time for my education chapter to begin. To me you were, are, Dad, and I am just so amazed at your life. You never burdened us with its tolls. I think I would have liked to know more but I trust your way, which I always have, and am content with what I know.

That was when you taught me about choices, which, once

made, had to be honoured. Having passed the all-England Eleven Plus exam, I was not sure exactly where we might be finally living, but I think Darlington was the first choice as it was central, with train and bus routes. And you gave me choices. I could be a day boy at Darlington Grammar School, a boarder at Sir William Turner's in Redcar, some 20 miles away, or a boarder at Barnard Castle, 15 miles only. At that time we didn't have a car and it transpired we never needed one. We looked at all options and made the trips, just you and me. Remember? You shared the histories of all the small towns and industrial towns we passed through.

And so we made the first major choice of my life. I would go to the same school as my brother; what younger brother wouldn't do that? You always believed in choices and the responsibilities that went with them. That was a great lesson, Dad. At this stage of life I have just reconnected with some old boys from Sir William Turner's. A couple of them remember Jim, and one in particular remembers when he started a fire from a burning cigarette in his coat. I'm sure you remember that incident – I think your military connection with the House Master saved him from expulsion!

While you had been a highly-respected officer, that did not define you. There was always a kindness, a sharing of knowledge and stories of history, a quiet pride in your family, country and county, your Yorkshire. You had patience.

As you know cricket was, still is, a passion for me. I was first introduced to it in its most basic form in Penang. I didn't know much about it, but it looked interesting. A couple of older boys came up with some wickets, a couple of bats and tennis balls we plucked from some tennis courts. Our first pitch was the lawn of the wonderful old Runnymede Hotel in Penang. The boys knew the rules, in a rudimentary fashion, and so we progressed and were occasionally encouraged by officers billeted at the hotel, who taught us the correct rules, how to bowl correctly and the skills of batting. And within a month or so, courtesy of Captain Gill, a whole new set of equipment arrived! Remember that? We boys were in our glory, and of course, given the shortage of people our own age, we invited girls in. We were ahead of our time.

Do you remember the summer you took me to my first real cricket match in Scarborough on the Yorkshire coast? We went to see Yorkshire play; they were without doubt the best team in England at the time with players whose performances are still held in awe today. You knew all about the players, pointed them out to me and had anecdotes about them all. Remember my thrill at seeing Fred Trueman bat and bowl? There was never any greater sight in cricket than watching that powerful body, hair flying, shoulders massive, ready to explosively unleash his potent weapon. In his later years as a raconteur and media celebrity, Fred described himself as "the finest bloody fast bowler that ever drew breath". Those greats that came after still hold him in reverence. Thought you would like that one, Dad.

One of the quietly taught life-lessons I learned on that trip was courtesy and politeness. I wonder if you recall it. The bus which went over the North York Moors to the coast made occasional stops to pick up and discharge passengers. Scarborough was a big draw that day as it was in the midst of their town festival, which was centred on cricket. Halfway there, two ladies got on; no seats. You immediately got up, took me to one side and offered the ladies our seats. Why? Because that was the thing to do. I never forgot that lesson. It was just so natural. Courtesies still existed.

As you know I immersed myself in the game at school and did well. You introduced me to my first club in Darlington, where I started league cricket. Then when I left home and worked in

Leeds and Nottingham, the game was truly part of life. Winter nets in Leeds, three to four games a week, and the same again in Nottingham. You know Dad, I don't think you saw me play except for a game in Nottingham. Long after you died Mam told me you used to watch all my games held in Darlington. You apparently used to walk down to the ground, take a quiet space and watch most of the game, not bothering anyone. She said you believed that to be my time, and there was no need for you to intrude or distract. Dad, even then you were considering others before yourself. Anyway I am sorry I didn't know that but I am glad to know it now. You were the quiet man, pleased and content with what you saw. I hope I gave you cause to smile from time to time.

Do you remember that night in 1957 when you took me out into the long back garden on Barmpton Lane in Darlington? There were no lights around us from streets or other houses, and we were alone with the night sky of northern England. You had me look up at the night stars in a specific direction and they seemed to grow in number the more I stared, one here, ten more over there. You quietly said "Don't move your head, just keep focused in the one area and relax. Blink if you have to". What I was really looking for was the one star that would be moving and leaving the others behind. And then I saw it. "Sputnik!" Man's foray into the universe. We just gazed, silent. That was a once in a lifetime experience, and you made it happen. I can see us still in that garden.

Well Dad, you will be pleased and no doubt proud to know that my shoes, even though more casual these days, are still kept clean. I am long past the time of wearing dress shoes, but perhaps I do miss the drilled-in routine of "spit, polish, shine". It became part of our DNA; did we have that way back? I would watch you clean and polish your hand-crafted boots and shoes with an impeccable routine. The habit of course was followed up with Jim. He was almost mesmerising in his routine. First the shoe for his good, normal leg. And then the extra care for the built-up shoe which had holes through the side-heels that allowed his leg-iron to clip in. It was part of his "I may be crippled, but check out my shining shoes, smart clothes and that immaculate Windsor knot in my shirt" mantra. These habits have followed me through life and certainly memories of you and he are not be far away when it came to the spit and polish part of the job.

What can I say about books? Having lived as long as I have, I can't say that I have read as many as you consumed. I have a picture of you, Jean and me at the Big House, in Port Dickson, Malaya, sitting in our armchairs, each of us with a book in hand. I learned early, and there were always boys' adventure stories or some annual of history and geography. You taught me well. Jean at her home in Scotland, just her now, always has a book within reach. She reads in quiet time over breakfast. There will be a book on her table; that oak table made by Jim, by the fire for an afternoon and evening read. And when she gets her bed warmed for the evening, she makes sure the book is by the bedside.

You never got to see her home in Berwickshire, but the bookcase in the drawing room is about twelve feet long with three shelves and packed with books. There are many in there that were yours, some having been read by me as they were classics of their time. Still are. There is a section with medical books, each signed on the inside by G. Gill MBBS. On the landing at the top of her long winding staircase are more shelves of books, many formerly yours, having reached you by way of Africa, India and Burma. In my own place here in Canada as I write to you, I have close to a hundred books, fiction, cricket, religion, history and biography. I think you would like many of them, especially those on our beloved Yorkshire and its great cricket players such as Brian Close and Fred Trueman, who were known to you.

You might smile at this one: a little old blue book, *The Book of Common Prayer*. On the inside, beautifully written is the following: "All Saints Northallerton Sunday School. Presented to Charles Gill, Christmas 1919, S.M. Thompson, Vicar". On the opposite page, again beautifully scripted, is a similar message: "The Church of St Matthew on the Plains, Burlington, Ontario. Presented to Alan Gill, Christmas 2002. Reverend Canon Carol Skidmore, Rector". Carol was a wonderful friend and also my priest.

I still enjoy fiction and non-fiction books in African, Indian, Malay and Chinese settings. Jean has told me of the ongoing parcels of books that followed you everywhere you went. One advantage of being a Quartermaster I suppose. Dad, I am so glad you quietly influenced me in my choices and opened up that wonderful world of books; their contents enrapture, educate, amuse and open up the mind. What a gift you gave to Jean and me.

What you may not have expected of me is that I have been writing a book myself. It is essentially made up of vignettes of early family stories and histories and doesn't really go past my most formative years. I wished I could have captured more from you but Jean, who in many ways was your confidante, has helped stir the pot. One you will know so well is the history we had with Bill Bangs, the rubber planter, spy, tortured prisoner from Singapore and the Burma Death Railway and close friend of the family. I recently came across some transcripts of his voice, recounting stories for the BBC, essentially bridging a seventy-year gap for me. I treasured those times he was with us. Thank you for the rides up the Kelantan River.

While you will remember that Jean and I, except for my first eleven years, have been separated by continents, we are close.

Northallerton and Malaya were the years when she and I spent the most time together. We can talk with ease and cherish what we were given as an example of how to live one's life by the love of our parents. There was also a special bond between you and her, and it is through her I have learned so much more about you; that prompt in turn has resurrected good memories from our lives together. We learned respect for others, the less fortunate, to see the good in others, to deal with what came our way with fairness and forthrightness, to honour duty and to know that your word is your word and that perhaps the unwritten mantra of "nihil nocere" was always present. The bar was high and occasionally I crashed it and have fallen to earth, but your mantra of "head up, shoulders back, forward march" has picked me up. She has certainly followed the rule, and as you know she lost Darien last year.

The time we had with you is cherished, albeit it short, as you were gone at sixty-nine. The hard wars and the early loss of Jim took their toll. She has quietly become the matriarch and with love and humour quietly reminds me that I am her much younger brother. Who would have thought at seventy-six I would be a much younger anything!

And so there are just the two of us right now, Jean in Scotland and me in Canada. We talk more frequently and the conversations will always have some reference to our parents and brother. We are bound still and I am committed, perhaps even needy, that I will see here at least once a year.

Well Dad, that was all overdue. It is a long time since those letters from boarding school were sent. I hope I haven't lost the touch.

Love you,

Alan

April 25, 2020

Herbie and Alan

Barbados Test Match

Alan. School Big Side, Top Left

Statue: Fred Trueman

Alan, Top Row, 2nd from Left

Gerald and Carol

Kathleen in carriage at Newcastle

Kathleen Plaque

Richard and Mario

Bill, Pam, Alan, Carolyn and Carlos

Runnymede Hotel, Penang

Runnymede Hotel, Penang

Darien   Jean

Jean and Spy, Port Dickson

Alan

Jean and Alan 2019

From the right, Carlos, Alan, Glenda, Carolyn, Sweetie, Pam, Bill

Bill, Alan, Carlos

Two Brothers, Carlos and Alan

CHAPTER 23

Vignettes

The hands of time had not changed him too much

I was born in 1452. I know, a long time ago. My family was rich, privileged even, and my education was well rounded with languages, history and physical activities. I also had a severe disability, a painful crippling scoliosis of the spine. I think that made me even stronger in my efforts to do well by people, those that I would eventually lead.

I had always been a man of integrity who cared for and respected his subjects. My rulings in law in my northern provinces were fair, and the population in that area were my greatest supporters. That Yorkshire blood still runs true today and many still consider me their legitimate king.

I was a good horseman and warrior, but my end was bloody as I was hacked and bludgeoned to death in the Battle of Bosworth Field on the 22nd of August 1485. It was not until 2012, some five hundred and twenty-seven years after my death, that the remains of my broken, twisted body was found, having been cast away into the ground near an old abbey. There was no dignity in my death, but now I lie in peace, in a place of honour, interred in Leicester Cathedral in England. My casket is crafted of good English oak and yew, as befits a king.

If there was any injustice towards me, it came from a man born almost 80 years after my death, a man whose precise date of birth is not known – what does that say? A man who at 18 married a much older woman and then abandoned her and their three children. A man whose licence with the truth became accepted history as he wrote his sycophantic stories to praise the monarchy that usurped my throne. These were the Tudors. This paid propagandist eked out his living on a tale of lies, having smothered my true history. He cruelly cloaked me as the hunchback, the crookback, a cold, calculating, deformed and unfinished creature, a murderer of young children. And as to that line "A horse, a horse! My kingdom for a horse!" He played it as if I wanted to leave the field of battle! How wrong and twisted was his writing. The call for a horse would have allowed my armies to see me in the field and lead them on to victory. It was well he came long after me. Vengeance I would have had, as I was a good warrior.

When you hear of these untruths you will doubtless now know that I am King Richard III of England, Richard Plantagenet, formerly Duke of Gloucester. It is comforting to know as I lie here, having finally received the last rites of my church, that there are many who love and respect me still. Through the centuries I have always been honoured by my northern subjects and for the last several decades there have been movements to discredit that obsequious, ingratiating, deferential literature hack of the Tudors known as Shakespeare. His stories are not about truth.

The hands of time have not changed me from the truth of my being. I am still the good King Richard the Third, known also as Richard Plantagenet. The truth has set me free from the scribbles and lies of that Tudor scribe.

Words

I love words. They are full of magic, hope, mystery and passion, and yes there are those that show us the darkness and fear. They come to us from far-flung parts of the world and include in my case Norse, Roman, French, German, Welsh, Arabic, Hindi, Persian and Old Malay. They form a base for our cultures and present common ground. But I digress; these elements are for the scholars and historians.

My take is simple. The love of words, their very being, captivates me. "Words" are different from "word", the latter being identified as a unit of speech. Who wants to be a "unit"? It is cold, scientific and calculating; where is the joy and romance in that?

From our words we get the potential to create. Words together are powerful, they multiply as they are speedily spoken or written, and become phrases, sentences, paragraphs, pages, chapters and books. Such a gift to us all. We peel away their meanings, unwrapping the gift from which flows the never-ending source of great storytelling. The words shout out "use us, create, share, learn, let your imagination run free, our source is unlimited".

What can we do with them? Take a group of people from all parts of the world with the common gift of sharing stories, written stories. Give them pen and paper and watch the explosion of ideas percolate. Memories go into overload, their pen or pencil scratches the paper and the words jump out, alive and racing to who knows where. The words fall on fertile ground and they grow extemporaneously. They demand attention and lead us we know not where.

How often do we start to write, the course of the story firmly charted, only to find that at the end, our destination, we have called into other ports, taken other ideas on board and following this diversion, eventually reach an uncharted destination. We are far better for those extended experiences, our words led us well. Our words do not allow us to be stale; we must be challenged.

I am excited every time I pick up my pencils, freshly sharpened, my pages blank. I breathe and allow the space to absorb me, and thus begins the tracing of black marks on their rapid, slanted journey along the lines. Racing faster, first one word and then the other. The flow develops and at times one can't stop until the thought is down. Trust your instincts, trust your instrument and honour the words that result. Do not look back. Mind, pencil and words will sputter forward, scudding over the waves to another unknown port. There will be a destination, identified by a new word, and the journey begins again. In fact it never stops. Exhilarating!

The Singular Pencil

I have learned that as my style of writing has matured over the years and I am now comfortable in its natural discipline, there is another element that is critical. A few years ago I wrote of the two forms of writing which I believe applied to me, and in turn I have made these a discipline. Of equal part to the content is the implement, our tool of the trade, that companion that allowed us to put words to paper. This summer I was struck by the importance of the role played by my chosen tool, the pencil, in allowing me to ply my absorbing craft as it spears forward, ever forward in flight.

This summer we decided to take a short trip from our lakeside summer home in Canada to visit our winter home in St Petersburg, Florida. This is in a quiet community, on the water, on the Gulf Coast. It is a gateway to whatever we wish to do and at a pace different to the quickness of the north. It is a smooth, easy place full of diverse interests and friends, with days bracketed by mesmerising sunrises and sunsets. The seasonal, short, swirling storms that rush through scatter freshness and the smell of the sea.

It is the calm quietness of the place that draws me. There are spaces, places to be found where there is no invasion except for the breeze, the wind in the trees, the birds and the warmth of the sun, as hot as you wish. It is that peacefulness that allows the mind to calm, change direction and free those percolating thoughts which become stories. A good atmosphere.

The time was ripe, mind and body ready as I prepared for my first day of writing. And then an immediate and mind-numbing panic. Where is my leather pencil case, the comforting home to a dozen or so black Tombow 2B pencils, sharpened, ready to lead and free my mind and thoughts wherever they may go? Missing!

I could remember sharpening the pencils, placing them in the case, all facing the same way, ready to be packed before the journey. Suitcases were checked and rechecked, other bags torn apart. Nothing. Panic, fear. The pencils had missed the flight! I had other pens specially chosen, fountain pens that allowed the black ink blood of life to flow through them unlike the passionless plastic sticks that are normally scattered around. I had my computer. None of these have the feel, the trust of the black Tombows that encourage, even drive, the free flow of thoughts. They know how to glide across the pages revealing the stories of life. Pencils have a comforting feel, they are a family, lined and laying together, of different lengths but sharpened and ready to support each other as they move forward. They are outnumbered by the cold keys on a keyboard which only receive the fleeting touch of finger tips, with letters well removed from each other and at no time make a bond with the hand that guides them. Those keys have no life. They are not on a journey, there is no touch, feel, caress in their black imprints.

This was a difficult start to my hoped-for peaceful escape into the land of words. I stuttered along with some pens and the desktop, but the energy was not flowing.

Day three came around, punctuated by the thought that "I must have a pencil somewhere, how can I not?" All the drawers were checked, living room, bedroom, kitchen, and the desk. The search was repeated. Nothing, Anxiety kept a hold.

Later in the afternoon I was looking for some batteries and found them in their dark cylinder uniforms, lined up in a draw. My hand stopped at a flash of light. Lying between the batteries, wearing black, thinner but longer, was a solitary pencil. The light had caught the gold embossed stencilling on its side, flashing the words 'Highest Quality Tombow'. Relief. Euphoria. All the senses of welcoming a long-lost friend were flowing. The day took on extra brightness, the burden was lifted. Life all around had new dimension, angst retreated and creativity was set free.

My singular pencil has done such stalwart, unselfish work. I have completed three vignettes, of which this tribute is but one. The pencil is much shorter now, its length perhaps reduced by one third. It has been unstinting in its tasks, which under more normal circumstances would have been shared by a dozen already sharpened pencils at the start of a day. There would have been companionship in the old leather case, their resting place. There would be stories to tell.

It has been the best of weeks.

The Uninvited Guest

I cannot, as with most of my life, recall my gestation or birth. I have no memory of when I first made a recognisable impact on my world. What I do know is that I have made a significant march to be at the forefront of a human life in the last twenty years. I am a force to be reckoned with; I win some, I lose some, but when I seep unknown into the conscience then I am there to control, for a while at least.

There never was, nor is there now, a pre-determined plan for me to make an appearance. In fact "appearance" may be a misnomer, as it denotes a required physical state. Perhaps "presence" is more encompassing, in that it is there but it is not visible. Yes, I like presence. I can suddenly announce myself by saying "I am here". I make an immediate impact, stir up the thought process, disturb the equilibrium of daily life. Where I was once dormant and paid no mind, I now rise up like a stallion hoisting its knight in armour, lance at the ready, charging forward into battle to create fear, havoc , pain and the death of tranquillity. Brutal shock is something I am sure I can conjure up time and time again. While I can cause this pain, I have no feeling of guilt or memory that it was I who actually created the situation in the first place. I don't think this is denial, even though I have no emotion. It is just what I do. Right or wrong. In fact I can't even tell you what right or wrong are; feelings, demons, forces of good or evil come to mind, but there again I don't know what these are either.

I do hear many repetitive words associated with my unannounced arrival. Wounded, pain, throbbing, creeping, invasive, vice-like, pending, battle, striking, blinding and so on; like the debris of the battle field springing to life. Doubtless in the human psyche or ethos I am not admired at all. But as you may surmise that does not register with me emotionally. It just is.

I mentioned earlier a time interval of 20 years ago; not quite a generation. This was the point of my great leap forward, perhaps not as magnificent as that leap forward in human evolution, but I suppose that depends on subjective points of view. My leap was not of my own creation but rather the result of the flawed nature of humans and their disrespect for one another and their codes. Apparently there is a code that states it is criminal offence for a human to drive a car at 50 miles per hour into the back of a stationary car stopped at a red traffic light. Strange people.

That was my moment; my impact. From then on I was to be a daily player in the life of my Human. I was up there in the Head where it all happens, close to Brain and Memory. What a thrill, I think, as that is an emotion, and an awakening. Brain, where Thought resides, was now my controller. Brain is interesting; it is the always ready, always thinking driving force of all humans, not just my Human. Test any human and say "stop thinking" – they can't. It is impossible. Brain also has Memory, which every human claims as their own, "my memory". How little they know! Memory, the library of everything, is their very own Google store of the good, the bad and the ugly. But Brain is still in control.

Brain has recorded my birth. Since then I have been the target of the voices and thoughts, the clarion cry for things that have come to be associated with me. Straining, distress, wounded, battle-worn, weighed down, brutal, vice-like, pulsating jack hammer, crushing and so on. Confusingly, Brain, of which Willpower is part, fights against me. There may also be something called 'stubborn attitude'. They all refuse to give in. But I know I can jump out and close everything down in my Human. If I could feel emotion, maybe I wouldn't like all these bad words, if that is what they are. Humans are to blame. It is not my fault that nerves get twisted and crushed, soft tissue has disappeared from spine and neck. I merely send the signals. I do not have my own brain, but I am part of Brain and Body. As I said earlier, I win some, I lose some. But I am not allowed to be the outright victor.

There is a battle going on. I am not sure if I win by the increased frequency of my presence, intensity and the creation of discomfort but I, or rather Brain, do get pushback. Meditation, medication and that well-worn British axiom "keep calm and carry on" are worthy opponents. Opiates for the soul mask my debilitating effect. My Human pushes on or may rest; and occasionally the awareness of my presence is dulled. My Human is certainly worthy of my challenge, but is he winning? I have not yet found a way around this and I don't know if Brain is working on a solution for me to do my job. It may be the opposite. There is also the unknown, something called Soul. It may hold sway over everything and there have been rumours that when Brain and I no longer exist, Soul will march on, the battle over and thus the victor.

To this point in my existence I have seen many changes. With the human population explosion, my 'kind' – I'm still not sure what we are – have increased on the same growth curve. We have been far ahead of humans in that we have always treated the male and female of the species equally. We were even at work in the non-gender specific group even before they knew they existed. I have also experienced an exponential growth in business due to politics. The 'kumbayahism' of the left is screeching louder than ever and I am grateful for that, if I can even feel that emotion, as I have seen a rapid rise in my work and I deliver with power. I am putting in more and more appearances; such validation. Then the Right's metaphoric guns are drawn and battle ensues and here I come. I rule!

Brain made a significant observation on Brain's own two

hemispheres, the left and the right. The left is responsible for logic, the sciences, order, and reason. The right controls creativity and art. I believe if the two political human political poles knew this I would be a force twenty-four hours a day. They would not know who they are or where they stand, and their thought processes would be even more tangled. I will be unstoppable.

Brain has even reasoned that I have been responsible for the increasing growth in pharmaceutical sales, opiate use, and the never-ending search for that cosmic interaction provided by marijuana or the myths associated with it. All the more business for me, according to Brain. And until lucidity and feeling return to our humans, then I will float like a butterfly and sting like a bee – a giant bee.

Well that about sums it up. I am not driven to divide and conquer, I am gender neutral. Embrace any human event that gives me presence and I will be with you wherever you are and as long as you live. You can count on me, you will not be abandoned. I am yours for the rest of your life. I am sure someone, here right now, can feel my presence. If you can't then Brain will surely deliver me to someone by the end of the day. Brain is king; Brain does not even feel pain, being much too busy telling every part of you what to do. Brain gets to write the music, conduct the orchestra and you get to dance.

So here I am. Who am I? I am HEADACHE! and I am yours forever until Soul takes over. May we have a long life together. You will always know when I am present.

The Battlefield

The battlefield before them was flat terrain, spotlights highlighting the background green, the inner space covered in blood-red with swaths of black touching all areas. Off to one side, the finely tuned wheel of the machinery was quickly whirling, a staccato chattering as the ammunition rolled to find its final target; there were thirty-eight possible landing spaces.

The final command was accompanied by a defined hand movement and was soft but clear, "No more Bets!" The wheel spun, the ball landed, some chips were raked in and a few remained to be augmented by the calculated odds of payout. The roulette game was in progress, and the odds never change. The participants were varied, male, female, aged roughly between forty and eighty plus. Facial expressions were tight or relaxed, in perpetual motion, and all eyes were fixed on the target as the ball dropped.

The eighty-five-year-old man proudly wearing his Marine Veterans hat, body comfortable but bent with the dignity of well-earned age, was sitting at the end of the table. His eight piles of one-hundred-dollar chips were neatly arranged, ten high. He had come a long way in his battles, starting out with ten chips. His 17 to 1 splits had worked gradually and there was the occasional payout on the 35 and 38 to 1 chances. A good evening, he'd won the day, victory!

He was about to leave when a young man in his early forties, neatly dressed, hair tidy with a few gelled green highlights and on his feet a pair of Nike high tops emblazoned with red and blue stars and stripes, saw the vacant seat next to the veteran and said "May I sit next to you sir?" There was a nod, accompanied by a smile. The newcomer sat, erect in bearing. He sat out the first spin of the wheel and organised his chips; twenty-five dollar values against his fellow combatant's hundreds.

Before placing bets the young man looked at the veteran and said, "May I shake your hand, sir? My family and I thank you for your service". The veteran obliged; how many thousands of times had he been thanked? He was always grateful for the acknowledgement. In his mind he played it forward to those who had sacrificed with him, but had never again seen home. There was a quiet, friendly feeling between the two men from different generations, they won, they lost but the wins were greater than the losses. As they cashed in they agreed to meet again the next day, to fight as comrades in arms.

The vet pushed himself up, straightened as much as the bent, weary body would allow and turned as his younger partner stood. There was a loud bump, a sound of solid on solid, as the younger man swung round and pushed himself up from his chair. Ever sharp, the veteran looked down and saw the state-of-the-art carbon-fibre prosthesis fitted above the knee and all anchored by the proud US-themed Nikes. "You served?" he both questioned and stated.

"Yes sir!" the younger Marine replied. "Five tours completed and I deploy next week for the sixth".

The veteran held the gaze of the Marine and stiffening as much as he could, saluting, said "Thank you for you service, son".

Ever faithful, they met again the next day; another battle to be fought and won together.

A style of our own
With apologies to William Strunk and E.B. White

My Writers' Group is an eclectic band of wordsmiths who share their trials and tribulations in their crafted stories. They have no fear of language and its many constraints, ploughing on to their promised land in the revelation of themselves and their stories, knowing they have conquered the laws, rules, regulations and inhibiting fears that the great god Grammar may have thrown in their way.

The names that may have struck terror in our hearts were short – Strunk and White. In 1920 William Strunk, a professor of English at Cornell, self-published his very short book called *The Elements of Style*. Covered were the eight elementary rules of usage, ten elementary principles of writing and a nod to misused and misspelled words. A gospel was created. Fast forward to 1957, when E.B. White, a former student of Strunk, updated the booklet and created what we know today as Strunk and White's *The Elements of Style*. You can't have one without the other. Again it was a small book that became more than the gospel.

This was the holy grail. Style or language becomes almost mathematical with some of its equations, such as the use of parallel construction and parallel concepts. Moving from mathematics to the discipline of law, we are faced with the admonition to omit needless words, use the active voice and strictly follow the laws of punctuation and grammar. Political correctness also wove its way into the dictates by suggesting that one should avoid unintentional emphasis on the masculine.

We know language and writing are forever changing. Our common language came in a large part from the precision and structure of Greek and Latin and was gradually transformed by the old French and English. It continues to ebb and flow, the tide ever changing.

Strunk and White is a good read, almost one hundred years on from its first self-published birth. It can be both amusing and challenging, and is certainly educational. White has a great exhortation which should be of encouragement to us all:

"Vigorous writing is concise. A sentence should contain no unnecessary words, a paragraph no unnecessary sentences, for the same reason that a drawing should have no unnecessary lines and a machine no unnecessary parts. This requires not that the writer make all sentences short or avoid all detail and treat subjects only in outline, but that every word tells. There you have a short, valuable essay on the nature and beauty of brevity — fifty-nine words."

I recently shared some of my stories, my vignettes, with a close and dear friend. Among her many attributes is her skill in organisation, no matter what the demands. In her working career she was the glue that kept the executive suite running without a hitch and her secretarial skills perfected the written words that lasered their way to their destinations.

Her first feedback – one knew this was the big cannon – was not about content, the heart of the words, the story, but of punctuation. What comma or how many go where, too many semi-colons, don't start a sentence with "and" or "but". Sentences too short, sentences too long, can't capitalize the first letters in mother or father and so on. She said she had taken the liberty of marking the offending letters, words and punctuation marks with pencil. After a reread, perhaps some of the original structure could stay. There was debate over too short and too long.

I did listen and later reread the apparent offending pieces in their pencil-modified form. That was followed by reading again several times the original version, which was the telling of a story with its flows and ebbs. The voice, whether spoken or in the head, is important. It is vocal and evokes passion and involvement. In the critical, rigid structure of the taught grammar the prose can lose life. Every word must tell, have its place, its freedom and cannot be fenced off. The exercise was useful, especially as my writing was still partially in raw form, and the minor edits helped.

I have just finished reading "Darkest Hour" by Anthony McCarten. It is a brilliant book that brings the lion, Winston Churchill, to the fore with his oratory and his written words;

the latter are themselves another form of seductive, beguiling oratory. McCarten himself leans into the power that Churchill demonstrated so often, the power of words and the delivery of context. I quote McCarten:

"Churchill, in late May, after a great deal of vacillating, of hemming and hawing, of all night pacing, of mental disorderliness, saying one thing and then the other, of an infuriating overuse of the volte face, of soul-searching, of headfulness, of listening, of reconsideration, of option-weighing, of reckoning, of black-dog speechlessness, was able to confront the nation and offered words toughened in the fires of intense doubt, and came down on the right side of history.

He got it right."

One sentence of eighty words, sixteen commas and one period, followed by the second closing sentence of four words.

The author ends his book with: "That May, Winston Churchill became Winston Churchill."

We are story tellers, we are language. Speak loudly, speak often, breathe life into words and allow the creativity of style to carry that life forward.

Two Women: Black and White Sketch

A living sketch; a moment captured of a silent agreement between two women. Their posture is erect, they sit primly, eyes focused behind perched rimless glasses. The glasses themselves accentuate both that primness and their body language signals; but of what?

They have a book or paper in their hands, but of what do they disapprove so disdainfully? They have exhaled their exasperated sighs and their just audible "tut, tuts".

I wish my older sister was here. I am sure she would zero right in, razor sharp as she is. There would be immediate clarity. Her mind would slip back to those convent days in our Malaya and she would agree that the education was outstanding. But if something was not quite right, if the pupil had not delivered accurately, indeed perfectly, the result was "the look", accompanied by sighs of exasperation. No comment of a positive "you can do better" but rather a stern "not good enough." It was if Sisters Agnes and Rose were joined at the hip. Their bearing, looks, frowns, and perfectly-placed glasses were all synchronised into a single movement.

The artist is certainly not my Sister but is a kindred spirit in sharing her own experiences from all those years ago.

"And then the room fell silent."

There was an inpromptu 10-minute exercise where we had to immediately start writing using the above phrase at least once and then share it with the rest of the writers.

My old boys' school in the north of England was a place of great tradition, learning and sports. Boys will be boys, and as with any class we would rush into History, the quieter ones to the front and the more disruptive reclaiming their stake at the back, chattering as they took their places.

Our teacher, S.E.T Hodgson, or SETH as we affectionately knew him, was a slim man, silvery white hair, round glasses, book in hand, wearing the traditional black robe, and he would watch us silently as we took our places. He had a quiet, calming aura. Coming out of the Second World War, he had been a distinguished and decorated officer. He had returned to his first love, teaching and shaping young minds. Through the bustle of boys settling in, he would turn and face the front wall and blackboard, his back to us. I can hear him now with a soft power in his quiet speech, saying, "Gentlemen, if you are not in the first three rows you will not hear me. I have done my share of fighting and shouting in another arena. This battle is up to you."

And then the room fell silent.

Privilege

A very close friend of mine was outlining to me how I had led a life of privilege in Malaysia and Trinidad, not quite understanding that living in a war zone (Malaysia at the time) and respecting the tenet of being in a country by an approved work permit, signed and renewed by the Prime Minister (Trinidad), did not constitute privilege just because I was white. His take on privilege was different in referring to British autocracy in Malaya and being in a senior management position in Trinidad. Based on that I had to be one of the elite, and that utterance comes from a lack of understanding of the role that people can play in their communities, no matter where they are in the world. It is a myopic view of the world of which people know less and less as their experiences become filtered through media and only the media of their choice. It is the new disease of myopianism.

What I do know that he was right for the wrong reason. Yes, it was a privilege to be a resident of both these countries and become educated by their people, history, geography, festivals, religions, politics, love and form personal relationships that are thriving today. I am privileged to have had those opportunities and am a better person for it. The one thing I do not have is myopia; I also subscribe to the treatise that "a little knowledge is a dangerous thing". The latter is too prevalent in our society.

CHAPTER 24

A WRITER'S FAREWELL

March 2018

In the summer of 2017, as with most summers, I was at our cottage on the lake in the Muskokas of Ontario. That is the place where I can dive into the peace, the tranquillity and the freedom to create, totally enveloped by nature. My pencils, ever sharpened, raced unhindered in my journals.

Last week we all had an enjoyable gathering in sharing our stories with our fellow residents at Point Brittany. Maureen capped off the event by her wonderful expose of who we are, how we coalesce, create and step into that brave new world of writing. She spoke of who we are as individuals and as a group. It was a caring piece. As I listened to her reading I was struck as to how closely her feelings, expressions and experiences were aligned with my own. Interesting how we were both inspired, almost a year apart, to reach out with the same thought process.

Here is an extract, the introduction to a longer piece which

I wrote in that July of 2017. I share it now as a salute to you, my fellow writers, my companions in the universe of words and expression, as some of us start to wend our way to other points of the compass to explore and then return.

I wrote of us:

"I am privileged to be a part of a writers' group, an eclectic coalescence of wonderful people, full of the tales of life, from all corners of the world. Such experiences from continent to continent. All that has been needed for the telling of those stories is the safety of an encouraging and supportive forum. The kindle has been lit and the fires of tales to stir the imagination keep on burning. Who are we? First and foremost we are story tellers. And hidden in our minds are the obituaries of what defined us to the outside world; the dentist, the lawyers, the health care providers, the bank executive, the preacher, the musicians, and yes that myriad of educators who stirred so many minds. Here also are the leader, a renowned and accomplished author driven by the theatre and the written word; those that supported families; the intrepid homemakers without whom we would be shallow and then we have the Artists who can capture it all. We are an interesting group. We overlap, we blend. There are other group dynamics and friendships outside of the writers; we all have other gifts, talents and these too are shared in forums that provoke, examine and fulfil us."

We are all better for having made our journeys, no matter the paths we took. They all lead to the same place, that haven that allows us to venture on to other worlds of fiction, facts, memories and life, all tied together by the gifts we share, plus the friendly discourse we all provide.

In John Irving's book *Cider House Rules*, Dr Wilbur Larch, brilliantly played by Michael Caine, delivers a closing blessing each night to his orphaned charges. It is powerful in its simplicity and has always stuck with me:

"Goodnight you Princes of Maine
You Kings of New England."

What a wonderful way to say goodnight!

AND SO
To you all I say
Farewell you poets, scribes and raconteurs
You creators, you guardians of words and memories
Until our next dawn.

What would it have taken to answer the last letter you wrote?

What would it have taken to answer the last letter you wrote or even make a phone call of response and support? That is the one question we'll never know the answer to, but perhaps we can imagine our lives would have changed forever and you would be here today.

How often do we troll through the "what ifs" of life? We will never know, no matter how much we dream and let our unfettered imaginations take control. It is what it is, and whilst that may sound cold, it is nevertheless fact. There is no going back, reimaging or reimagining life on a different road. Losing touch is quite definitive and can be the end of something that was wonderful and blossoms no more.

Who we are today, in the now, is different to who we may have been had we not lost touch and allowed the magic, the electricity, to die. It is like a molecule that separates and then attaches to create something new. The original connection has been broken.

How can I have the sadness of losing touch, when life has continued its march regardless of our choices? We travelled different roads, it was not meant to be, the roads did not meet again. But wait! There are memories. If we were to meet tomorrow would that spark, that thunderbolt, still strike? Would you still be the old you? Would I mirror that? Would we put a meaning to the lost years from where we stood then or from where we stand now? In calling them "lost", we have already applied a label. It is true that the meaning we assign to something provides the emotions in our life.

To always think it sad that we lost touch is mundane, unrealistic. It is what it is.

As I am today, there are times when I walk down a busy street anywhere in the world and I see a tall blondish lady, hair bouncing, exuding that certain something, alluring, moving with ease, a quiet power. I can't see the eyes but am sure they are blue, and my mind slips, perhaps pulls me back, through the many decades ago when she was in my life, perhaps even *was* my life. That is what I treasure and live with, and the resurrected memories cannot be sad.

Covid: defeated by memories and DNA

Who would have thought that the topics of isolation, separation, segregation, quarantine, seclusion and paranoia that dominate our lives today would allow a warm, caring telephone call, full of memories, to take place? This Sunday I called Jean in her remote village in the Scottish borders. It is more remote in the winter months when the snow blows in and there may be no access for a number of days. Check it out, the name is Longformacus.

Jean, recently widowed after a marriage of sixty-four years, is alone. Yet she is not. The post lady calls in daily on her long route to check on her and use the washroom. Neighbours, distant behind the beautiful natural stone walls and flourishing trees, make sure lights are being switched off and on and most importantly that all the curling smoke can be seen coming out of the chimney of the drawing room on an evening. But it is an adjustment, with the partner of a lifetime missing.

She fondly quotes our father, that quiet gentleman, the soldier who served his country with distinction through various wars: "Shoulders back, head up, forward march!" And so we moved on. She was in good spirits, coal fire glowing and crackling and her one small glass of wine in sight, yet to be sampled. Her memory goes further back than mine as she lived through the Second World War. The family took in refugees from London. Mother, with three children to look after, also had to work at night and Father at that time was in India and Burma.

She recounted a story of one of the German bombing raids. Mother pushed us all, and I was carried, into a dark cupboard under the stairs and we huddled together, covered with blankets. No light except for a flashlight, to be used sparingly. My brother was hit on the head by a hard object and shouted. Mother firmly told him not to make such a fuss! The offending object turned out to be a precious jar of raspberry jam. We survived.

Jean and I, in our partly overlapping generations, are fortunate. We went through those difficult times. Our early life also strengthened us, as we were raised in an Asian country away from the so-called comforts of our homeland, away from family and friends. We learned from different experiences. We have the DNA imprint of our parents and grandparents, who were challenged by two world wars and industrial strife. There were rules in place which were for the good of the many; they were followed.

Today's challenge in the world is not just a pandemic but how we, as people, deal with it. Can we give up lifestyle choices for the good of the majority? The "Me" generations have been sheltered from what shaped the generations for the first fifty-plus years of the twentieth century. Can they rein in what they take for granted and join the fight, follow the rules and turn selfishness into selflessness? Is this their Road to Damascus? We are all in this together – or are we?

From the Dark Side

Let's see. Who do you know that made a bold statement that resonates with you and occasionally chills you to this day? It is also relevant. Here it is, immortally etched in your mind by the great Jack Nicholson: "I'M BACK!"

You know me. I have been around for millennia. I'm known by many names. Names carved in history, your minds and beliefs. Some names I've cherished, others, as with the more modern ones, are weak and meaningless. They do not define the true darkness that is within.

Some of you will know me from having read the "good" book and followed its dictates. I'm not too sure what good has to do with it. Let me take you back. Remember "Exodus!" Your ancestors were overcome with all sorts of joyless and at times deathly experiences. Too many to mention them all, but here are a few hints. Remember the River Nile turning to blood, pestilence and plagues of frogs, lice, boils, flies and so on. The phrase I thought really catchy was the Plague of Locusts. It wasn't as destructive as some of the others, but I liked the sound. Oh and course Darkness, of which some say I am the Prince.

Let's jump to other recorded histories which surely you know about. The mid 1300s, the Black Plague; I liked that. As your ancestors started to explore the world they went to unknown territories from Europe and the Middle East to Asia. On their return they brought back viruses and gradually eliminated one third of your tribes. What's wrong with you people? Eventually, after five to ten years the pestilence died off. Or did it?

In the 1800s there were problems all over the world. You couldn't even keep your water clean. Thanks for helping me!

Then in the early twentieth century, when you were all annihilating each other with your wars, you killed twenty million people and wounded twenty million more. You call that maturing as a species? As if that was not enough, along came the Spanish flu, which took another fifty million world-wide. What's wrong with you people? Or should I say gleefully from my personal perspective, "What's right?"

Your last hundred years has seen ebola, SARS, Hong Kong flu, Asian flu and swine flu, to name a few pesky irritants. And of course you played war games throughout the century and managed a pretty good total of seventy-five million killed and wounded in World War Two. And here we go again another pandemic, another panic, a thinning of the herd.

You know and I know that this pandemic will pass. It may take time, but it will pass. I say it will take time as there are always groups among you who will shrug their shoulders and not follow your codes for the betterment of all. This is a weakness in your human race.

I am not sure where I will leave the matter, but it does seem you have many so-called leaders who have no substance. I don't need to step in and sow the seeds of doubt as they are doing a fine job by themselves. But I do know I will need a vacation to the Dark Side, and that is when you will come through this, in my absence.

Oh, and I should say I don't like my new name "Covid 19". What is this? Some Disney/Hollywood movie production? Give me a break! I need something darker and a new calling card from Jack Nicholson "I'll be back!"

I think I'll stick with "The Prince of Darkness".

Handwriting: a personal journey

Handwriting has three forms, to be complete. If there are more I do not know. It is physical, a code, that follows the format our thoughts and inner selves dictate – and then comes the decoding. How did my particular style develop its form, its organisation into a finished product that appears to others and is decoded by their differently-wired brain?

As we humans progress, we shed some of the old skin and the clear form dissipates like ripples on a puddle which once existed as still reflective water, but when touched spreads its waves until the sheet is blank once again and awaits a further engraving.

We learned our basic code, the letters, the numbers, the identifying qualities, the exact upright military bearing of the 'i's', the 't 's', the vertical trunks of which are enhanced by design of half circles which make the earlier lettering into a 'b', a 'p', a 'd' and so on. And then there were the links that joined the letters which gave us the fullness and appearance of a word; our world of communication was now open.

There were rigid laws. All letters in a word were joined by hoops, and it was only at the end that the writing instrument could be raised from the paper and dot the 'i' or cross the 't'. The law could be broken of course if the word was long and the pen needed to quench its thirst by being raised from the paper and dipped into the ink. But we are human and we can only follow rigidity for so long. We are lazy yet creative and we cast aside the old code that was the model. We personalize and modify our strokes, as does the artist with brush in hand, and ultimately we become identified by our writing style. At that point the reader will know who formed the word; no need for our Picasso-like sign off.

And so I come to me. What is my code? Can others break it? What does it say about me?

I like order, but I do not like statue-letters standing to attention. I slope with a leaning to the right. I have kept some of the mechanics, but most have been thrown out. I have developed a flourish, or rather the letters have, depending where they sit in the formation of the word with particular attention to what came before and what comes after. My word is not formed by leaving the instrument on the paper until the word is complete. Taking the word 'its', the letters are not conjoined and then the pen or pencil raised to dot and cross. No. Rather there is a bold vertical stripe, the pencil raised and a second downward vertical stroke made, raised again and slashes across the top of the second letter (now we have a sword) and that top lateral swipe forms the top part of the 's' with the curve completed below. Dramatic! The cut and thrust of a sword fight as I slash my way through a paragraph.

I have blended the individual print of letters from my early childhood, followed the path through youth and adulthood with the cursive restraints and have boldly added the piquant sauce and flourish of calligraphy. My style gives me free and passionate rein as my thoughts and words tumble out and are once captured with the passion they deserve. My trusted, sharpened charcoal Tombo 2B pencils are the tools that never let me down; they are a key component. A pen or the organised letters of a keyboard are inadequate. My pencils and my style mix well and give me comfort in writing. They appear to acknowledge me, they are eager to be set free and never tire.

A childhood adage comes to mind, a greeting written in a book some sixty plus years ago: "Thoughts are the tools of mind. Be a good mechanic". The pencils are a key component.

BV - #0078 - 160322 - C23 - 229/152/15 - PB - 9781861519832 - Gloss Lamination